Ultimate
ORCHID

Oncidium macranthum
'PATIENCE', AM/AOS

DK

Ultimate
ORCHID

THOMAS J. SHEEHAN

IN ASSOCIATION WITH
the **SMITHSONIAN INSTITUTION**
and the **AMERICAN ORCHID SOCIETY**

Paphiopedilum henryanum
'HALEY SUZANNE', CCM/AOS

London, New York,
Munich, Melbourne and Delhi

DK PUBLISHING
Book Designer: Mandy Earey
Project Editor: Ray Rogers
Art Director: Tina Vaughan
DTP Designer: Russell Shaw
Production Manager: Chris Avgherinos
Publisher: Sean Moore

CONSULTANTS
American Orchid Society: James B. Watson
Smithsonian Institution: Thomas Mirenda

Cymbidium lowianum var. *lowianum*
'COMTE D'HEMPTINNE', CHM/AOS (*p.* 36)

First American Edition, 2001
04 05 10 9 8 7 6 5 4 3
Published in the United States by
DK Publishing, Inc.
375 Hudson Street
New York, New York 10014

DK Publishing, Inc. offers special discounts for bulk purchases for sales promotions or
premiums. Specific, large-quantity needs can be met with special editions, including
personalized covers, excerpts of existing guides, and corporate imprints. For more
information, contact Special Markets Department,
DK Publishing, Inc.,375 Hudson Street, New York, NY 10014
Fax: 212-689-5254.

Library of Congress Cataloging-in-Publication Data

Ultimate Orchid / Smithsonian Institution, American Orchid Society.
p. cm.
ISBN 0-7894-6128-5 (alk. paper)
1. Orchids. 2. Orchids—Varieties. 3. Orchids—Pictorial works.
4. Orchid culture
I. Smithsonian Institution. II. American Orchid Society.

SB409 .U48 2001
635.9'344'0222—dc21
00-065816

Reproduced by Colourscan, Singapore
Printed and bound in Slovakia by Neografia

See our complete catalog at
www.dk.com

CONTENTS

Foreword 6

ORCHIDS IN HISTORY 8

WHAT IS AN ORCHID? 10

ORCHID CLASSIFICATION 12

VARIABILITY 14

*Phragmipedium
longifolium*
'LEXIE SAUER',
AM/AOS (*p.* 28)

PART
ONE 16

PAPHIOPEDILUM
ALLIANCE 18

CYMBIDIUM 34

ONCIDIUM ALLIANCE 40

CATTLEYA
ALLIANCE 52

PLEUROTHALLIDS 68

DENDROBIUM 76

VANDA ALLIANCE 86

PHALAENOPSIS
ALLIANCE 98

BOTANICALS 110

Indian stamp

ПОЧТА СССР 1991

Russian stamp
(p. 152)

Aerangis
curnowiana
(p. 136)

Masdevallia
veitchiana
'MACRO',
AM/AOS

PART
TWO 138

CONSERVATION 140
MEDIA AND POTTING 142
PROPAGATION AND BASIC CARE 144
WHERE TO GROW ORCHIDS 146
PESTS AND DISEASES 148
ORCHID SHOWS AND AWARDS 150
COLLECTIBLES 152

Glossary 154
Index 156
Acknowledgments 160

background: *Christieara* LUANG PROBANG 'CHARLES BOLICK', AM/AOS

FOREWORD BY THE
SMITHSONIAN INSTITUTION

I t's undeniable. There is something uniquely captivating about orchids. Revered and cultivated centuries ago in China, passionately coveted in Victorian Europe, and avidly nurtured by millions worldwide in the 21st century, orchids connect to the human psyche in powerful ways. Recognizing this, in 1974 the Smithsonian Institution began to build – with a mere five orchid plants and a talented and influential committee of staff members – what was to become one of the best orchid collections in the world. As a result of the generous bequests of many donors, the collection burgeoned to more than 30,000 plants in less than ten years. Also, the Smithsonian's role as rescue center for endangered species has enabled many strange and unusual orchid species to grace our greenhouses. While necessity has pared down our collection in recent years, those that remain are among the finest orchid species and hybrids, many of which are unavailable in the trade.

Today, orchids from this venerable collection feature prominently in the many horticultural exhibits throughout the Smithsonian's 11 buildings in Washington, DC. It is hoped that, by displaying these fascinating plants to the public for their edification and enjoyment, we will perpetuate the ageless enthusiasm they inspire and capture the imagination and intellect of the next generation. Our children, after all, will be the stewards of our planet and its denizens. We consider it an important part of our mission to captivate them with the amazing diversity and beauty that exists within the orchid family.

Brassocattleya
BINOSA
'WABASH VALLEY',
AM/AOS, from the
Smithsonian Institution
collection

Thomas Mirenda
Smithsonian Institution
Orchid Collections Manager

FOREWORD BY THE
AMERICAN ORCHID SOCIETY

The Smithsonian Institution: a byword for excellence in preservation, conservation, and education. The American Orchid Society: the essential source of information about the culture of the fabled flowers that inspire a passionate band of aficionados. Professor Thomas J. Sheehan: scientist and lifelong educator, whose lucid and practical approach to orchids has encouraged the novice grower and challenged the enthusiast for decades. The combination of these institutions is an unbeatable alliance.

For more than 80 years, the American Orchid Society's information-dissemination activities have reflected the interests of its membership and the greater orchid community. The study of orchids, their propagation, preservation, culture, care, and development evokes a passion among

Minutes from the first meeting of the American Orchid Society, held April 7, 1921

hobbyists that is insatiable. The pages of *Ultimate Orchid* – with its quality photography and text that is scientifically sound without being technologically intimidating – will doubtless be frayed and worn from use by countless orchidoholics.

What is the mystique of orchids? What passions drove the collectors of yesteryear to risk life and limb, and still lures today's hobbyists? What challenges drive newcomer and old hand alike in this fabulously crafted family of plants? *Ultimate Orchid* will provide you with some of the answers and guide you to a most pleasurable avocation. Enjoy and catch the fever.

Lee S. Cooke
Executive Director
American Orchid Society

ORCHIDS IN HISTORY

John Lindley (1799-1865), early orchidologist

Orchids and people have had a long and colorful relationship over the centuries. Because of their worldwide distribution, orchid species have been sources of medicine and food for many cultures for thousands of years. The age of exploration witnessed the transfer of orchids from their native lands to orchid enthusiasts around the world. Growing orchids for their beauty, and bringing them together in breeding programs to create new hybrids, has become a major floral industry and hobby for thousands of devotees.

EARLY REFERENCES

The history of orchids since 600 BC is fairly well documented. Confucius (551-470 BC) referred to *lan* (the Chinese name for orchid), stating it was the "King of Fragrant Plants" and making numerous references to "the supreme fragrance of *lan*." According to Confucius, having the aquaintance of good men was like entering a room full of *lan*.

The first use of the word "orchid" is attributed to Theophrastus (370-295 BC). He used the Greek word orchis, meaning "testis," undoubtedly a reference to the pair of underground tubercles found on many Mediterranean orchid species. Pliny's Natural History (AD 77), the origin of the Doctrine of Signatures, in which it was believed that God indicated the usefulness of a plant through its appearance, referred to the sexual power of orchids. Also in the first century AD, the Greek physician Dioscorides indicated that orchids were useful for treating genital problems.

Confucius

Vanilla flavoring is extracted from the fermented capsules (seed pods) of various species of Vanilla. Shown here are the flower and the immature capsules.

ORCHIDS FOR EATING

In 1552, the Aztec Herbal, also known as the Badianus Manuscript, included the first reference to vanilla, indicating that this extract from the capsules (the seed pods, or "vanilla beans") of Vanilla planifolia and other species was used to flavor a beverage made from cacao (chocolate). Vanilla (tlixochitl in Aztec) also found use as a perfume and as a body lotion. It was believed that this lotion not only relieved fatigue but also gave strength to overcome fear and render the heart strong.

In 1633, the tubercles of Cynorkis were discussed in Gerald's Herbal: "These kinds of Dogs stones be of a temperature hot and moist, but the greater or fuller stone seemeth to have much superfluous windinesse, and therefore being drunke it stirreth up fleshy lust."

Around 1640, John Parkinson also addressed the properties of Cynorkis by referring to the Doctrine of Signatures and stating that "Dioscorides saith that the roote there of being boyled is eaten as other sorts of bulbes are, and that if men eate the greater, they shall beget men children, and if women eate the lesser they shall bring forth women children. And if the women of Thessalye give the soft roote in Goates milk to procure lust, and the dry roote to restraine it and the virtue of one is extinguished by taking the other."

BRINGING THEM INTO CULTIVATION

The earliest known importation of tropical orchids occurred in 1731, when Peter Collinson imported Bletia verecunda (now B. purpurea) into England from the Bahamas. Other orchids began to arrive, and by 1794, there were 15 species of tropical orchids growing in the greenhouses at the Royal Botanic Gardens, Kew.

It was not until 1812, when Messrs. Loddiges established the first orchid nursery in London, that orchids became a commerical crop. Among the species Loddiges imported was a plant of Oncidium bifolium, to which there was a note attached, reading "it was hung up in the cabin without earth and continued to bloom during the greater part of the voyage home," a statement that then was regarded as a traveler's tale and beyond the limits of credulity.

While collecting in the Organ Mountains of Brazil in 1818, William Swainson came across some plants that were not in flower, and Swainson apparently did not think highly of them. However, since they were stiff and leathery, he used them as wrappers for other plants he shipped to England. The bundles were received by Mr. William Cattley, a horticulturist. He became interested in the unusual plants and decided to tend them. One of the plants flowered in November 1818 and looked like nothing Cattley had even seen. Dr. John Lindley agreed the plant was new to horticulture and named it Cattleya labiata (see p. 54) in honor of its rescuer and in recognition of the large floral labellum (lip).

STARTING TO GROW

The date of when tropical orchid species were first imported into the United States is not known for certain. Some historical accounts indicate that the first major shipment of orchids was received by Mr. John Boott of Boston in 1838 from his brother James in London. However, other evidence seems to indicate that John Boott may have cultivated orchids as early as 1829. Also, a Mr. Wilder placed an Oncidium flexuosum on the display table at the Massachusetts Horticultural Society meeting on June 27, 1837, almost a year before Boott's shipment arrived.

The Sander family in England was one of the earlier large orchid growers. Their collectors sought out orchid plants worldwide and sent them back to England. In 1894 they employed around 100 people just to pot the orchids being shipped in and had around 2,000,000 plants under their care.

ORCHIDS IN COMMERCE

Commercial production in the US began around 1848, when Charles Power started his establishment in Framingham, Massachusetts. Thomas Young set up his operation in Bound Brook, New Jersey in 1905 and soon became the largest grower of cut orchid flowers. In 1911, Armacost and Royston opened their business in California. These growers reportedly had more than 100,000 square feet devoted entirely to orchids by the early 1920s.

Hawaii has been often called "the Orchid Isles," even though orchids were not among the earlier importations to that tropical climate. Bananas, sugar cane, and pineapples were staple crops by the early 1920s; it was not until 1930 that Y. Hirose, in Hilo, began to import a wide selection of species,

This woman is processing orchids for leis, the flower garlands that are a traditional gift of greeting in Hawaii.

initiating what was to become an important agricultural industry for the islands. The first cut flowers were shipped from Hawaii in 1942. Within the next eight years, Hawaii became the world's leading commerical orchid-growing center.

THE MODERN ORCHID

The discoveries of aseptic seed germination by Louis Knudson in the 1920s, polyploids and their role in breeding in the 1950s, and meristem propagation in the 1960s have all had a significant and stimulatory effect on orchids and orchid production. These discoveries have enabled growers to produce hybrids faster and in greater numbers than ever before.

Rows of glass flasks contain mass-produced orchid plantlets grown under ideal sterile conditions.

WHAT IS AN ORCHID?

Despite the enormous variety found among the approximately 25,000 species and more than 110,000 hybrids, all of the members of the orchid family are related to each other by their flowers. The five main characteristics common to orchid flowers are: 1) zygomorphy; 2) the column; 3) the rostellum; 4) two or more pollinia, and 5) the labellum (lip).

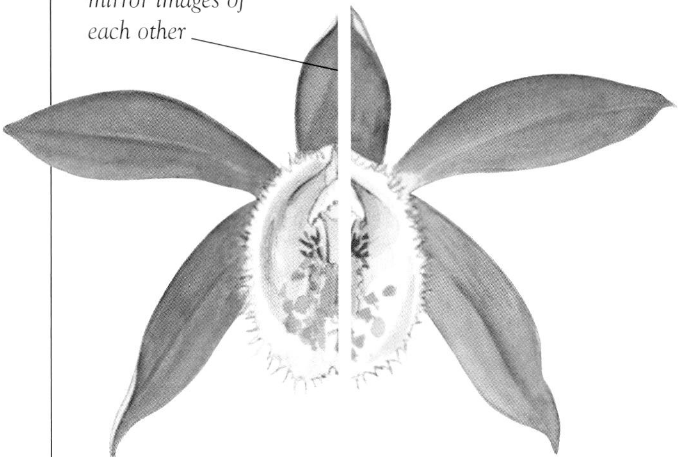

Pleione formosana (p. 126)

Petal (orchid flowers have two)

The two halves are mirror images of each other

Sepal

ZYGOMORPHIC FLOWERS

There are two main flower shapes in the plant kingdom. Zygomorphic (irregular) flowers (such as orchids) can, in face view, be divided in half along one plane only. In contrast, regular flowers (such as a rose) can be divided to produce two equal halves along any plane through the center.

COLUMN (GYNANDRIUM)

Orchid flowers have an uncommon reproductive system. Instead of having separated stamens (male parts) and stigmas (female) as in lilies and roses, orchids have a structure called a column. The column is a fusion of the male and female portions of the flower. The column is usually waxy and white and lies in the middle of the flower, sometimes almost hidden by the folded-over side lobes of the labellum. In some orchids (such as *Phalaenopsis*; see pp. 99-109) the column may be the same color as the petals.

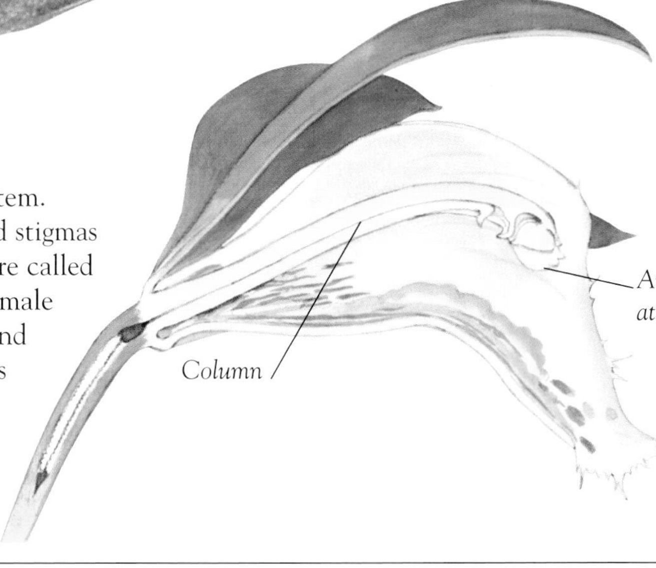

Anther cap at tip

Column

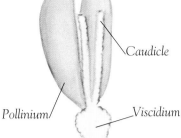

Sepal (orchid flowers have three)

Pollinium

Caudicle

Viscidium

Petal

Sepal

Labellum

POLLINIA (SINGULAR POLLINIUM)

In the majority of flowers, pollen, the powderlike male reproductive cells produced by stamens, rubs off when something comes in contact with the blossom. Not so in orchids. The pollen in orchids is packaged into small masses called pollinia. They may be joined to a small stem called the stipe or caudicle, which in turn may connect to a sticky disk, called the viscidium, which readily attaches to and detaches from pollinating insects. The number and shape of the pollinia can be used to help identify plants: for example, the genus *Phalaenopsis* has two pollinia, *Cattleya* has four, *Laelia* has eight, and *Brassavola cucullata* has 12.

Anther cap

Rostellum

Pollinium

Pollinium

Rostellum

ROSTELLUM

The rostellum is a gland at the tip of the stigma that performs a twofold purpose in many orchids (for example, *Cattleya* or *Phalaenopsis*) It serves as a dam of tissue separating the male portion of the flower from the female, thus preventing self-pollination and ensuring cross-pollination. The rostellum also plays a very important role in pollination. As the pollinating insect enters and comes in contact with the rostellum, a bead of very sticky glue is laid down on the insect's back. This ensures that when the insect backs out of the flower the pollinia at the tip of the column will adhere to its back and be carried to another flower for pollination.

Side view of labellum

LABELLUM (LIP)

The labellum is a highly modified petal and can be the largest and most colorful floral segment (part). It often serves as the landing platform for the pollinating insect. In some orchids, the labellum is broad and almost flat (*Cochleanthes*, p. 118), pouch- or slipper-shaped (*Paphiopedilum*, pp. 20-27) or very tiny and hidden in a sepaline tube (*Masdevallia*, pp. 70-71). The labellum may be wavy and/or fringed and bear spurs (see *Aerangis* and *Rangaeris*, p. 136), hairs, and other structures.

11

ORCHID CLASSIFICATION

The first major system of classification of the orchid family was created by John Lindley in 1825. For 40 years he continued working, trying to hone his system to perfection. Over the years, noted taxonomists (classifiers) have studied and modified the arrangement of the orchid family. Presently, most taxonomists agree that Robert L. Dressler's work is the most definitive and so is widely accepted. The classification presented here is based on Dressler's *Phylogeny and Classification of the Orchid Family* (1993) and is reflected in the organization of this book.

FAMILY

Any group of genera (see next page) sharing the same combination of characteristics forms a unit called a family. There are more than 300 flowering plant families in the plant kingdom. Family names end in -aceae.

SUBFAMILY

In large families, genera (see next page) that are believed by taxonomists to have a common origin are grouped together into subfamilies. There are at least five subfamilies recognized in the Orchidaceae. Subfamily names end in -oideae.

CLASSIFICATION CHART

The chart on these two pages shows how a particular orchid, *Laelia purpurata*, and its varieties fit within the orchid family. Beginning with the orchid family at the top, successive levels further subdivide the groupings until arriving at the species and variety levels at the bottom.

Colors in the boxes of the various levels are keyed to the text descriptions above.

See pp. 52-67 for a detailed presentation of *Laelia* and its relatives in the *Cattleya* Alliance.

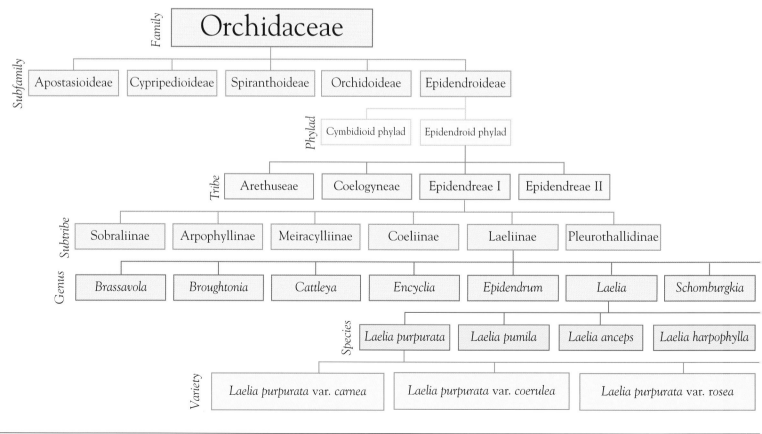

PHYLAD

This is a natural phylogenetic line (essentially a branch or limb of a family tree) containing a group with similar characteristics. Phylad names end in -oid.

TRIBE

The tribe is the next level down for sorting out large, complex families. It contains a group of genera that are more alike than dissimilar. Presently the orchid family is divided into 20 tribes. Tribal names end in -eae.

SUBTRIBE

The more similiar genera within a tribe are placed into subtribes; they may contain as few as one genus or have multiple genera. Dressler divides the Orchidaceae into 74 subtribes. Subtribal names end in -inae.

GENUS

A genus (plural, genera) consists of a group of plants whose common characteristics bond them together more to each other than to other members of the family. Taxonomists recognize over 800 genera in the orchid family. Genus names end in a variety of letters, often in -a, -us, and -um.

SPECIES

The species is the basic unit of classification in taxonomy. To date there have been more than 25,000 species named in the orchid family. Species names end in letters that "agree" with the genus name, as per botanical naming regulations.

VARIETY

Within a population of a species, an individual may be found that shows a minor difference that distinguishes it from a typical member of the species. For example, a white-flowered plant of a normally purple-flowered species would be a variety. The orchid family contains many named varieties.

——— ORCHID NAMES ———

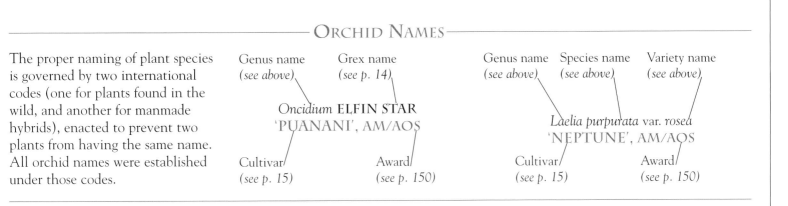

The proper naming of plant species is governed by two international codes (one for plants found in the wild, and another for manmade hybrids), enacted to prevent two plants from having the same name. All orchid names were established under those codes.

Genus name *(see above)* Grex name *(see p. 14)*

Oncidium **ELFIN STAR** 'PUANANI', AM/AOS

Cultivar *(see p. 15)* Award *(see p. 150)*

Genus name *(see above)* Species name *(see above)* Variety name *(see above)*

Laelia purpurata var. *rosea* 'NEPTUNE', AM/AOS

Cultivar *(see p. 15)* Award *(see p. 150)*

——— ALLIANCE ———

The term "alliance" is used to designate a group of genera that have many common characteristics and can be used for breeding to produce new hybrid genera. An alliance is limited to genera within a single tribe, for example the *Cattleya* Alliance, found on pp. 52-66.

Images in the photo galleries in Part One appear with the following location codes:

tl	*top left*	cr	*center right*
tc	*top center*	bl	*bottom left*
tr	*top right*	bc	*bottom center*
cl	*center left*	br	*bottom right*
c	*center*		

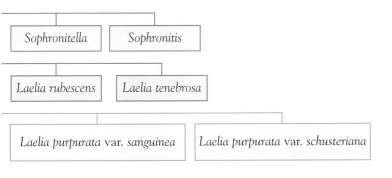

VARIABILITY

Not every individual within a given species necessarily produces flowers that are identical to the other flowers produced by other members of that species. Variability in appearance, which reflects underlying genetic differences, occurs both in nature and in cultivated plants. These differences from the norm can be appreciated in their own right, and hybridizers take advantage of variability in their breeding programs to produce new forms, colors, and other traits.

BOTANICAL VARIETIES

Laelia purpurata, a species native to Brazil, demonstrates remarkable variability. More than 25 examples of differences in flower color have been recognized and officially named as botanical varieties (see Classification, pp. 12-13). Many individual plants of these varieties have been further selected, named, and vegetatively propagated as cultivars, a few of which are shown here.

Also see pp. 52-53.

Sanguinea refers to the red-purple overall coloration of this unusually dark variety

Laelia purpurata var. *sanguinea* 'TWIN PEAKS', HCC/AOS

Coerulea refers to the blue shading on the petals and lip

Carnea refers to the deep pink (literally, "flesh-colored") lip

Laelia purpurata var. *coerulea* 'CRAIG REAVIS', AM/AOS

Note the bright yellow and purplish pink shades of this lip

The rich purple lip distinguishes this selection

Laelia purpurata var. *carnea* 'HOWE', HCC/AOS

Laelia purpurata var. *schusteriana* 'PURPLE VELVET', HCC/AOS

Laelia purpurata 'NEPTUNE', AM/AOS

GREX

Grex, a Greek word meaning "group" or "flock," is the term used for all the offspring of any given hybrid cross. After a hybridizer officially registers a grex name for a cross, all the plants produced from seeds of that cross (and identical crosses made later), plus any asexual divisions made from those plants, are members of that particular grex. Flowers of any given grex may be quite similar or show easily noticeable variability, as seen here with *Sophrolaeliocattleya* California Delight.

Yellow floral segments

The three examples shown here have similar, but not identical, lips

Orange floral segments

MULTIGENERIC CROSSES

Many orchids have several generations of hybrid crosses in their genetic background, sometimes involving as many as nine different genera. As each new genus is introduced into the lineage, an increase in the degree of heterozygosity (differences at the basic chromosomal level) occurs, multiplying the chances for visible differences to develop. This is the basis for the ever-broadening range of colors and shapes found in hybrid orchids.

Yellow-orange floral segments

A UNIQUE FAMILY

Among all the families in the plant kingom, the occurrence of scores of multigeneric hybrids is a phenomenon unique to the Orchidaceae. *Sophrolaeliocattleya*, the multigeneric cross illustrated here, results from the genetic union of three genera: *Sophronitis* (p. 66), *Laelia* (p. 58), and *Cattleya* (p. 54). Many other multigeneric hybrids exist in the Orchidaceae and are illustrated throughout this book.

——HYBRIDS AND CULTIVARS——

A hybrid is the result of the union, whether naturally occurring or manmade, of two plants of different genetic backgrounds. They occur principally on the species and generic levels (see pp. 12-13). A primary hybrid is produced when two species are brought together; the earliest manmade hybrids were all primary hybrids, such as *Cattleya* Hybrida (see p. 56). Bringing two genera together creates a bigeneric hybrid (such as *Laeliocattleya*, see p. 62), and three or more in combination produce a multigeneric hybrid, for example *Sophrolaeliocattleya*, as illustrated on this page. Over the years, hybridizers have combined existing species and hybrids to produce increasingly more complex and horticulturally desirable genetic combinations.

The term "cultivar" is the horticultural equivalent of the botanical term "variety" (see p. 13). It is used to identify a specific and genetically unique plant and all of its vegetatively propagated offspring (that is, not produced from seed but rather from dividing the plant into separate pieces or raising new plants from a cutting). Cultivars may be selections of naturally occurring (wild) plants or the offspring of two cultivated plants brought together by a bee or other pollinator, but in most cases a cultivar is the result of an intentional process done by a hybridizer. Many orchids shown in this book are cultivars and depict the finer qualities of their grex. Cultivar names occur in single quotes, such as *Phalaenopsis* Hilo Lip 'Lovely'.

PART
ONE

No other group in the plant kingdom

can match the incredible diversity

found within the orchid family

(Orchidaceae). The range of plant

forms and sizes, along with the far

greater variety found among the

colors, shapes, and sizes of their

flowers, dazzles anyone who takes the

time to investigate these marvelous

creations of nature (the naturally

occurring species) and their manmade

progeny (the hybrids).

Angraecum leonis

PAPHIOPEDILUM ALLIANCE

The names of all four genera in this group are derived from the Greek word *pedilon*, meaning "sandal" or "slipper," giving rise to the common name, slipper orchid. These plants occur worldwide: *Phragmipedium* and *Selenipedium* are found in the New World tropics,

Cypripedium parviflorum var. *pubescens* grows from Alaska to Newfoundland and south to North Carolina.

Paphiopedilum is native to the Old World tropics, and *Cypripedium* occurs on all continents in the North Temperate Zone. By far the most popular genus of this group is *Paphiopedilum*. Most of the early *Paphiopedilum* hybrids were large, full, almost round flowers, nicknamed "bullfrogs" or "bulldogs" (p. 24), in which the flowers occurred mostly in shades of brown, green, and combinations of the two. The last quarter of the 20th century witnessed a new array of colors entering the picture, particularly after the introduction of several yellow- and pink-flowered species from southeastern Asia and southern China (p. 22).

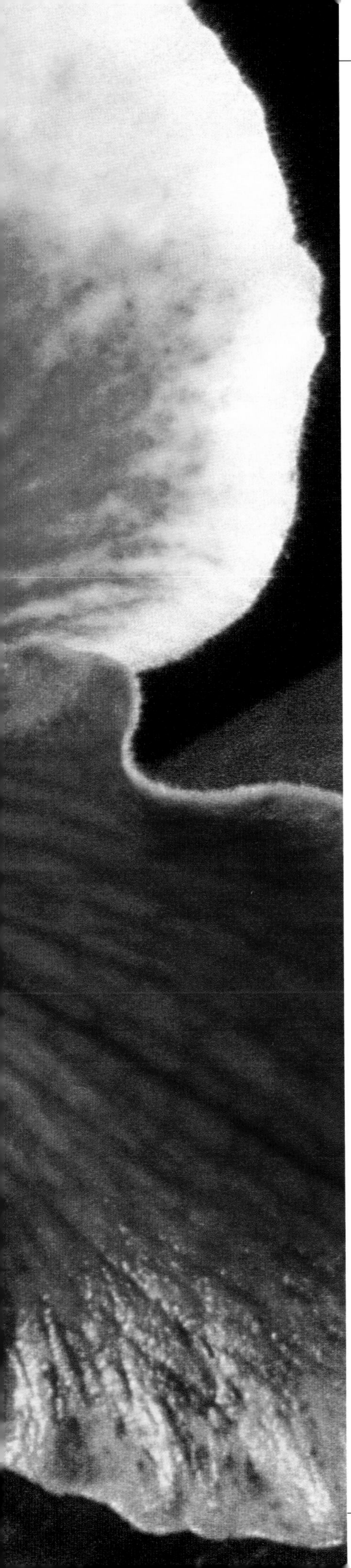

Paphiopedilum BOURNHILL
Registered in 1976, this hybrid has sired a number of offspring.

PAPHIOPEDILUM SPECIES I

The nearly 50 species of *Paphiopedilum* are native to woodlands from the Himalayas to the Philippines and south to New Guinea. These very popular and widely cultivated plants are able to grow in a wide range of temperatures. Most bear a single long-lasting flower per stem, but a few produce multiple blooms per stem. Of note in this group is the synsepal, formed from the fusion of the two lateral sepals and occurring behind and below the lip. In some species (for example, *P. sukhakulii*), the lip obscures the synsepal.

The species name venustum *alludes to the goddess Venus, revered for her beauty*

Paphiopedilum venustum
Here is the first *Paphiopedilum* species described and introduced into cultivation, c. 1820. Many variants have since been discovered and named.

MULTIFLORAS

Paphiopedilum philippinense
This very attractive species from the Philippines usually bears more than one flower per stem.

Paphiopedilum victoria-regina
Although it can produce up to 32 flowers per stem, this species rarely has more than two flowers open at a time.

Paphiopedilum rothschildianum **'FLYING WINGS', HCC/AOS**
First discovered in 1887 and named in honor of Baron Rothschild de Ferdinand, this striking species is rare in nature, known from only three locations on Mt. Kinabalu in Borneo.

The chisel-shaped lip points out rather than down, the latter being the more common position

GALLERY

tl *Paphiopedilum fairrieanum* var. *album* 'GRANNY SMITH'

tr *Paphiopedilum ciliolare*

c *Paphiopedilum sukhakulii*

bl *Paphiopedilum villosum* 'GOLD MOON', HCC/AOS

br *Paphiopedilum insigne* var. *sanderianum* 'GLADIATOR', AM/AOS

PAPHIOPEDILUM SPECIES II

The warm-growing species from southeastern Asia are deservedly popular, not only on account of their flowers, but also because many have beautiful mottled foliage. The introduction of the Chinese paphiopedilums of the Parvisepalum group in the 1980s greatly increased their popularity and provided exciting new genetic material. The interesting and unusual species shown here have been widely used by hybridizers (see pp. 26-27 for some examples).

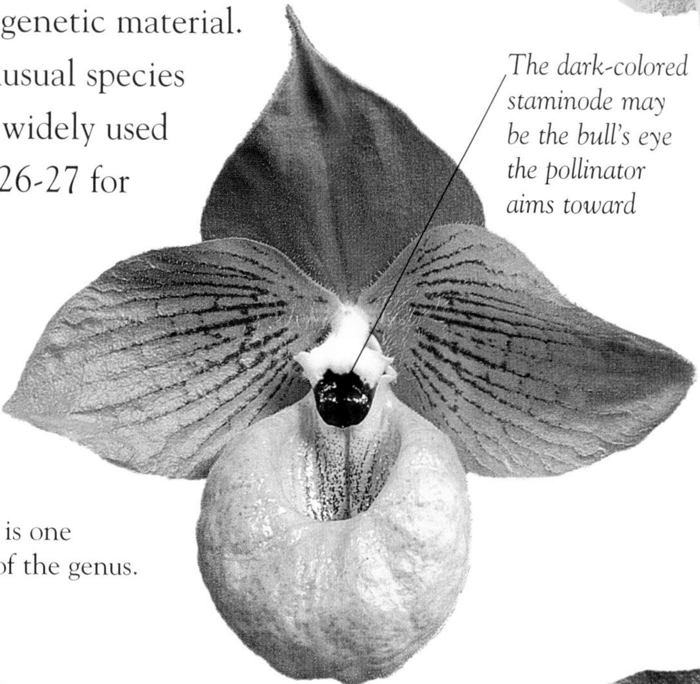

The dark-colored staminode may be the bull's eye the pollinator aims toward

Paphiopedilum malipoense
'BRONSTEIN-WALSH', AM/AOS
This species from Malipo (in southwest China) bears the greenest flower of all the Chinese paphiopedilums and is one of the few fragrant members of the genus.

Paphiopedilum armeniacum
'SOLAR MAX'
The name tells it all: here is the Venus slipper (*Paphiopedilum*) that is orange-yellow (*armeniacum*). It grows naturally in Yunnan, China and was first described in 1982.

The staminode is a distinctive identification feature

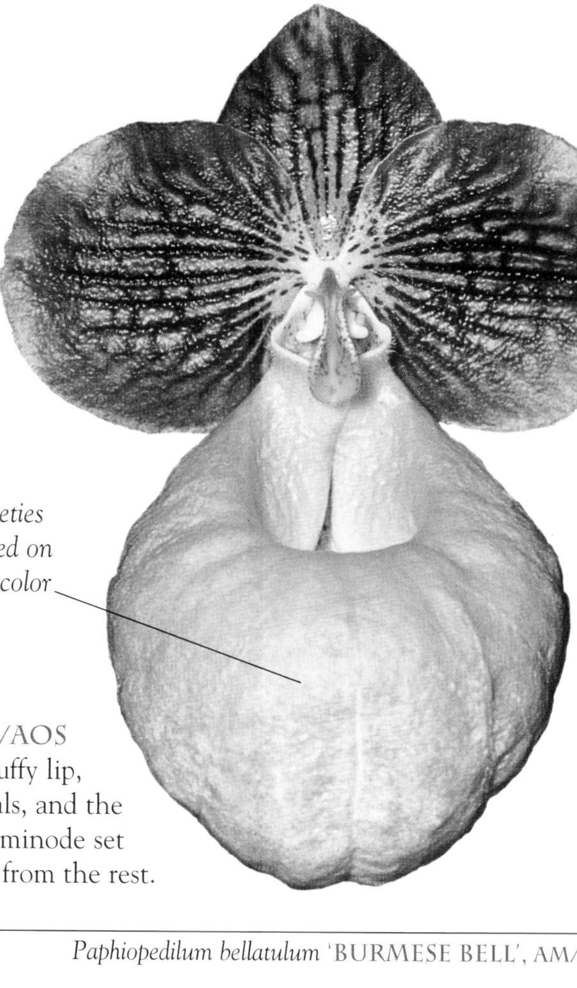

Some authorities recognize four varieties of this species, based on flower size and lip color

Paphiopedilum delenatii **'JILLIAN'**, HCC/AOS
Only a few of the first plants of this species introduced into France in 1913-14 by army officers returning from Vietnam survived. Now this species thrives in cultivation after being reintroduced from the wild in 1972.

Paphiopedilum micranthum
'AFTON', FCC/AOS
The very large, puffy lip, the thin, flat petals, and the unique yellow staminode set this species apart from the rest.

Paphiopedilum bellatulum 'BURMESE BELL', AM/AOS

PAPHIOPEDILUM HYBRIDS I

Veitch Royal Nursery in Chelsea, England, the first to produce a hybrid *Paphiopedilum*, created *Paphiopedilum* Harrisianum, a cross between *P. barbatum* and *P. villosum* (p. 21) in 1869. Since then, hundreds of hybrids have been created, and they are still being enthusiastically produced and grown today. Depicted here are hybrids typical of modern breeders' endeavors. The ultimate goal of many hybridizers is to produce flowers that are nearly round in outline and almost flat, except for the lip.

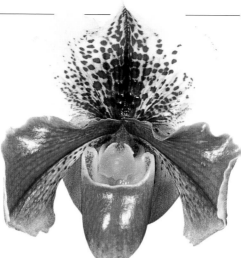

Paphiopedilum
SANDRA BAY
Many *Paphiopedilum* hybrids show a sharp contrast between the dorsal (upper) sepal and the other flower parts.

Paphiopedilum **BETTY BRACEY**
'MEADOWLARK', HCC/AOS
Although registered in 1956, this grex is still being used to produce new hybrids.

Staminodes vary widely among these hybrids

Paphiopedilum
GREEN GOLD
Although by no means a full, rounded flower, this 1969 hybrid is still a popular parent.

Breeders strive for a flat dorsal sepal, as shown here

Paphiopedilum **GREEN WINDOW**
'STONE', AM/AOS
Another relatively new hybrid (1996), it shows the color combination that dominated this group in the past.

Paphiopedilum **ANJA**
'PENNY', HCC/AOS
This full flower was bred in 1982 and is used often as a parent today.

Paphiopedilum **IRISH EYES** 'HALEY SUZANNE', CCM/AOS

PAPHIOPEDILUM HYBRIDS II

The creation of new *Paphiopedilum* hybrids took a dramatic turn during the 1980s, when the Chinese species became readily available to hybridizers. Their bright colors and puffy lips made possible a new array of hybrids. These, coupled with the warm-growing, mottled-leaved southeastern Asian species, such as *Paphiopedilum callosum* and *P. bellatulum* (p. 23), completely revitalized interest in the slipper orchids.

The lip shape is intermediate between those of its parents (see the caption below)

Paphiopedilum **PETULA** 'ELAINE'S BOOBOO', HCC/AOS
Although first bred almost 50 years ago, this is typical of many warm-growing hybrids being released today.

Paphiopedilum **DOLLGOLDI** 'GOLDEN GIRL', AM/AOS
It's easy to see the influence of *P. rothschildianum* (p. 20) and *P. armeniacum* (p. 22) on the shape and color of this flower.

The sepal resembles those of both of this hybrid's parents

Paphiopedilum **IANTHA STAGE** 'SUPER'
Paphiopedilum rothschildianum (p. 20) provided the lip, and *P. sukhakulii* (p. 21) contributed the petals of this showy hybrid.

The influence of P. micranthum is evident all over this flower

Paphiopedilum **MAGIC LANTERN** 'ROSE GLOW'
Crossing *P. micranthum* with *P. delenatii* (see p. 22 for both parents) produces this intense strawberry color.

Paphiopedilum **GARY ROMAGNA** 'WIZARD'S FAVE'

PHRAGMIPEDIUM SPECIES

Most of the tropical New World slipper orchids belong to this genus, first described by Robert A. Rolfe in 1896. Although many have only one flower open on a stem at a time, the stem may produce flowers for up to a year (for example, *Phragmipedium longifolium*). Curiously, while the flowers of most plants wilt and fade away, an entire *Phragmipedium* flower drops off while it still looks fresh. Grow these at intermediate temperatures and keep the medium constantly moist.

Phragmipedium besseae
'EAT MY DUST'

Phragmipedium besseae
Amazingly, this brilliantly colored species from Peru was not discovered until 1981. Its introduction led to the production of an array of colorful new hybrids (p. 30).

Phragmipedium besseae var. *flavum*
'SUNDANCE'

Phragmipedium longifolium
'LEXIE SAUER', AM/AOS
It's not uncommon for a well-grown plant to be in flower every day of the year. This species has sired a number of excellent hybrids, including *P*. Sorcerer's Apprentice (p. 30).

Distinctive staminodes are helpful in identifying species

Lip color varies among members of this species

Phragmipedium besseae
'APRICOT'

— PETALS STAND OUT —

One of the most interesting features found among *Phragmipedium* species is the great variation found in the length of their petals. They range from the short, broad *P. besseae* type and the narrow, slightly longer *P. longifolium* shape to the droopy and twisted type found in *P. pearcei* and *P. caricinum*, to the extremely long, twisted petals of *P. wallisii*.

Phragmipedium pearcei

Phragmipedium caricinum

Phragmipedium wallisii 'WHITE RIVER CASCADE', HCC/AOS

Phragmipedium wallisii 'WINTERGREEN'

PHRAGMIPEDIUM HYBRIDS

Until recently, *Phragmipedium* hybrids bore flowers that were in combinations mostly of greens and browns, although a few hybrids made with *P. schlimii* had some pink coloration. When *Phragmipedium besseae* (p. 28) entered the picture, a vastly different group of hybrids arose, and today the majority of the colorful hybrids have *P. besseae* genes in their background.

The lip shows the influence of P. Eric Young (see right)

Phragmipedium DON WIMBER 'PENNY', HCC/AOS
This flower resulted from backcrossing *P. besseae* (p. 28) with *P. Eric Young*, itself a child of *P. besseae*.

The lip recalls a grandparent, P. schlimii

Phragmipedium **ELIZABETH MARCH 'LOVELY'**
The dominance of *P. Sedenii* as a parent is evident in the flower shape, but the improved color comes from *P. besseae*.

Phragmipedium **JASON FISCHER 'PHOENIX RISING', AM/AOS**
This flower is three-quarters *Phragmipedium besseae*. Its other parent is *P. Mem. Dick Clements* (see below left for a hybrid from that grex).

THE INFLUENCE OF PHRAGMIPEDIUM BESSEAE

Phragmipedium **MEM. DICK CLEMENTS 'RICH RED', HCC/AOS**
Combining the genes of *P. sargentianum* (one of the parents of *P. Sorcerer's Apprentice*, right) and those of *P. besseae* results in shorter, broader, more erect petals and greatly enhanced color.

Phragmipedium **CHINA DRAGON 'ELEGANT'**
Here the hybridizer has mated a multiple-flowering, very long-petaled hybrid (*Phragmipedium Grande*) with *P. besseae*. The petals are shorter than in Grande, but the influence of *P. besseae* has greatly intensified the color.

Phragmipedium **NOIRMONT 'FIREBIRD'**
Crossing *Phragmipedium* Mem. Dick Clements (see left) with *P. longifolium* (p. 28) produces a flower with slightly narrower, more drooping petals than Mem. Dick Clements, and it deepens the color.

Phragmipedium **SORCERER'S APPRENTICE 'LOTHAR', AM/AOS**
This combination of *Phragmipedium longifolium* (p. 28) and *P. sargentianum* has flowers similar to *P. longifolium*, but the flowers of this cross are more colorful.

Phragmipedium ERIC YOUNG 'ETHEREAL'

CYPRIPEDIUM

The genus *Cypripedium* was first described in 1753 by Carl von Linne (Linnaeus). For the next 100 years, all orchids with bootlike lips were named *Cypripedium*, until the genus was divided into four genera (see p. 19) in 1886. The approximately 45 species are commonly called lady slipper orchids or simply slipper orchids. All are terrestrial (growing naturally in soil).

The puffy, soft, pouchlike lip suggested the common names

Cypripedium acaule
Found from Georgia northward to west of the northern part of Hudson Bay, the moccasin flower, or pink lady slipper, grows in a wide variety of habitats, usually in very acidic soils.

FROM EAST TO WEST

Cypripedium formosanum
'TRIDENT'S TWINKLE TOES', CCM/AOS
Note the pleated, sawtooth-edged leaf on this Taiwanese native, which inhabits open, moist locations and woodlands.

Cypripedium californicum
Native only to California and Oregon, this dramatic, clump-forming species grows near mountain streams in moist areas. It bears up to 12 flowers per stem.

THEY SPAN THE GLOBE

Cypripedium macranthum
This large-flowered species grows naturally from European Russia eastward to China and Japan, usually in damp locations, including open meadows and forests.

Cypripedium reginae
Ranging from North Dakota east to Nova Scotia, the queen lady slipper forms colonies on the margins of swamps, in prairies and meadows, and on wooded slopes.

Cypripedium fasciculatum (green form)
Oddly, this western North American *Cypripedium* is more closely related to Asian members of the genus than to its North American counterparts.

Cypripedium parviflorum var. pubescens

CYMBIDIUM

The genus *Cymbidium* was first described in 1799 by Olaf Swartz, who coined the generic name from the Greek word *kymbos*, "a boat-shaped cup," in reference to the shape of some of the flower lips. Cymbidiums have a long history of appreciation and cultivation, especially in eastern Asia. Toward the end of the Yuan Dynasty (1279-1368) cymbidiums were the favorite subject of Chinese painters. *Cymbidium finlaysonianum* flowers served as talismans to protect some Malay villages, and the roots were used to cure sick elephants. Today in the Old World, the variegated miniature species and hybrids are very much sought after, especially in China and Japan. Cymbidiums were imported into California from England in 1910 by Mr. Henry E. Huntington for his garden in Santa Barbara, California, and they are now widely grown in southern California as landscape subjects. California is also home to major commercial suppliers of *Cymbidium* cut flowers for spring holidays.

Cymbidium sinense
Although the flowers may be small in stature, they are borne in large sprays and emit a very strong fragrance.

Cymbidium **JOHN WOODEN**
'BRUIN', AM/AOS
Members of this grex make good garden subjects and are excellent providers of cut flowers.

CYMBIDIUM SPECIES

Cymbidiums are native to the western Pacific Ocean basin, spanning a vast area from India to southern Australia. Consequently, there are both warm- and cool-growing species. In the Northern Hemisphere, the cool growers bloom in time for Easter and Mother's Day. The plants are either terrestrial (growing in the soil) or epiphytic (growing on other plants).

Cymbidium lowianum
'CONCOLOR', CBR/AOS
This species honors Sir Hugh Low, who collected orchids in southeastern Asia and was the first European man to scale Mt. Kinabalu in Borneo in 1851.

Cymbidium hookerianum
'LOYOLA', HCC/AOS
Hailing from northern India and southern China, the 6in (15cm) nodding flowers bloom in late spring.

Cymbidium lowianum var. *lowianum*
'COMTE D'HEMPTINNE', CBR/AOS
More colorful than the related 'Concolor' (above), var. *lowianum* shows this species' typical flower color.

MINI CYMBIDIUMS

Cymbidium lancifolium
The species name refers to the lancelike leaves. Each flower stem bears up to six 2in (5cm) fragrant blooms. These attractive plants require little space.

Cymbidium kanran
'MAKINO'
In Chinese, *kanran* means "blooming in winter" or "cool-growing," giving a clue to how to grow this species.

Cymbidium sinense
The species name indicates this darker-toned beauty originally came from China. Tall, 32in (80cm) flower stems bear heavily scented, long-lived flowers.

Cymbidium erythrostylum
'MAGNIFICUM'
Erythrostylum refers to the red columnar structure in the flower's center. Flowers are borne on 24in (60cm) arching sprays.

Cymbidium canaliculatum (Queensland type)

CYMBIDIUM HYBRIDS

Hybridizers have been creating new cymbidiums for more than 100 years. One of the earliest hybrids was *Cymbidium* Eburneo-lowianum, registered by Messrs. Veitch and Sons of Chelsea, England in 1889. It resulted from a cross of *Cymbidium eburneum* and *C. lowianum* (p. 36). For some time, the majority of hybridizing efforts centered around the cool-growing types in an attempt to produce flowers with broader floral parts and a full, round flower form. However, during the last half of the 20th century, demand increased for warm-growing hybrids with larger flowers.

Cymbidium CRACKER JACK 'SANTA BARBARA'
This grex was popular in the 1970s, when it received several American Orchid Society flower-quality awards.

The column above the lip contains the reproductive structures

Cymbidium PHAR LAP 'RUBY GLOW', AM/AOS
The clear pink coloration, enhanced by the white picotee edge, has not gone unnoticed by AOS judges and home growers.

—— GALLERY——

tl *Cymbidium* **AFRICAN SKY** 'SAVANNAH', HCC/AOS

tr *Cymbidium* **VENTANA CREEK** 'HIGHLIGHTS'

cl *Cymbidium* **CHURCH CREEK** 'PAINTED LADY'

cr *Cymbidium* **CASTLE ROCK** 'ORANGE MAGIC'

bl *Cymbidium* **TARPY FLATS** 'JAZZ FESTIVAL'

br *Cymbidium* **MENDOCINO** 'SHAMROCK'

Cymbidium ORCHID CONFERENCE 'GREEN CASCADE'
Green-toned orchids are always popular: the color harmonizes with many other colors.

Cymbidium ROCKY POINT 'BROWNIE'
Not often found in flowers, brown can feature attractively in floral designs and color schemes in the garden.

Cymbidium MESCAL RIDGE 'CALIFORNIA'
Large, fuller flowers meet one of the standards hybridizers are striving toward to satisfy the cut-flower trade and hobbyists.

Cymbidium ELEANOR RIGBY 'HARMONY', HCC/AOS
The pendent flower cluster is typical of hybrids in which *Cymbidium devonianum* appears as a parent.

ONCIDIUM ALLIANCE

Odontoglossum
LAURA HETT
'SALMA', AM/AOS
The irregular spotting on the
flowers, with no two floral
segments appearing identical,
is typical of this group.

The Oncidiinae, the scientifically recognized name for this alliance, is a large and very variable New World group that encompasses more than 70 genera and 1,200 species of orchids occurring naturally from Florida south to Brazil and includes warm- to cool-growing genera. More than half of the species fall into two genera, *Oncidium* and *Odontoglossum*. Flower shapes range from the flaring, bright yellow "skirts" (the floral lips) of the dancing-lady orchids (*Oncidium*, pp. 42-45) to the large, pansylike flowers of *Miltonia* and its hybrids (pp. 46-47) in vibrant pinks, reds, yellows, and white, often with distinctive darker markings. Taxonomists frequently move some of these species from one genus to another. Consequently, in the officially published literature for nomenclature, species may be listed under one or several genera, and those names may well change in the future.

Miltonia
BEALL'S APACHE TEARS 'M'
The floral markings suggest an *Oncidium*
flower was superimposed onto this *Miltonia*.

ONCIDIUM SPECIES

This genus was first described in 1800 by Olaf Swartz, who coined the generic name from the Greek *onkos* (meaning "tumor" or "swelling") to describe the warty growths found on the lips of all the species in this genus. Note that some do not have the "skirts" typical of the dancing-lady orchids. Oncidiums are mostly warm to intermediate growers.

Oncidum baueri
This flower, borne in clusters on a much-branched inflorescence up to 10ft (3m) tall, has the typical color combination of many *Oncidium* species.

Oncidium leucochilum
Tall, arching, branched sprays produce a multitude of long-lasting, colorful flowers. The species epithet means "milky lip."

Oncidium hintonii
The flowers are only about 1in (2.5 cm) in diameter, but the plants usually produce multiple inflorescences, each bearing ten to 15 flowers.

Oncidum aurisasinorum
The species name refers to something gold or yellow, undoubtedly a reference to the flower color. This species belongs to the section affectionately referred to as the mule-ear oncidiums. Species in this group have stiff, erect, leathery leaves, one atop each small pseudobulb, which have been likened to a mule's ear. The leaves are usually borne in tight clusters.

Oncidum trilobum
'NANCY K', HCC/AOS
The two distinct side lobes on the lip inspired the specific epithet of *trilobum*. The rolled-back floral segments appear narrower than they actually are.

Oncidum sylvestre
'MID MICHIGAN', HCC/AOS
The flowers of this West Indian native have very distinct, yellow, tumorlike growths at the base of the lip, which are the basis for the name *Oncidium*.

Oncidium bifolium

ONCIDIUM HYBRIDS

The production of *Oncidium* hybrids got off to a slow start: by the 100th anniversary of orchid breeding in 1956, only 40 *Oncidium* hybrids had been registered, compared with 1,600 *Cattleya* and 4,500 *Paphiopedilum* hybrids by that date. The first *Oncidium* hybrid was officially registered in 1909, when Messrs. Charlesworth and Company produced *Oncidium* Illustre, a cross of O. *leucochilum* (p. 42) and O. *maculatum*.

Oncidium ELFIN STAR 'PUANANI', AM/AOS
This flower's lip vividly shows why many oncidiums are called dancing-lady orchids: it looks like the flaring skirt on a senorita.

The degree of spotting on the lips varies within the grex

The contrasting lip color adds to the charm of this hybrid

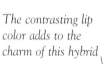

Oncidium SHARRY BABY 'SWEET FRAGRANCE', AM/AOS
Chocolate-scented flowers are displayed on upright, branched inflorescences.

Bumpy lip tissue (callus) is common in Oncidium

Oncidium GOLDEN SUNSET 'BRILLIANT'
The broad, flaring, speckled labellums (lips) are the major attraction of these flowers.

Oncidium CLOUD EARS 'TALL, DARK & HANDSOME', HCC/AOS
The size, shape, and color of this flower make it easy to identify it as an *Oncidium*. Note the lumpy growth (callus) on the lip, a common feature that suggested the genus name.

Oncidium GALVESTON BAY 'CHASE', AM/AOS

MILTONIA SPECIES AND HYBRIDS

Dr. John Lindley (p. 8) named this genus in honor of Earl Fitzwilliam, Viscount Milton of Yorkshire, England in 1837. The first grex, *Miltonia* Bleuana, was registered in 1889 and resulted from a cross of M. *vexillaria* and M. *roezlii*. *Miltonia* is native to Brazil, and the closely related *Miltoniopsis* is found from Ecuador to Costa Rica. All of their hybrids, registered as *Miltonia*, range from cool to warm growers and are cherished for their large, pansylike flowers. Like the related *Oncidium*, many show variation among the flower segments and from flower to flower, especially in the patterning on the lips.

The markings on the segments come from the M. clowesii parent

Miltonia **GOODALE MOIR** 'GOLDEN WONDER', HCC/AOS
Open flowers (those with space between the flower parts) in this group often are the results of *Miltonia flavescens* being in their genetic background.

Miltonia **ARTHUR COBBLEDICK** 'SNOWFIRE'
A major breeding goal, not only in this group but also in other orchid groups, is to have all the flowers arranged on the stem so each indivual flower is visible.

Spots are distinct on both sides of the petals

The dark spots a[t] the base of the petals are very common among Miltonia hybrids

Miltonia **JEAN CARLSON** 'ROSEMOON'
The popularity of these hybrids is due not only to the large size and superb color of the flowers but also to the attractive markings.

Miltonia **ROUGE** 'AKATSUKA', CCM/AOS
Patiently waiting for plants to grow to specimen size will reward the grower with spectacular flowering.

GALLERY

tl *Miltonia spectabilis* var. *moreliana* 'LINDA DAYAN', HCC/AOS

tr *Miltonia spectabilis* var. *moreliana* 'HARFORD'S EBONY STAR', FCC/AOS

c *Miltonia* **RAINBOW FALLS** 'RASPBERRY'

bl *Miltonia* **ROBERT NESS** 'HARVEST MOON', AM/AOS

br *Miltonia* **ARTHUR COBBLEDICK** 'STRAWBERRIES AND CREAM'

ODONTOGLOSSUM AND BRASSIA

The genus *Odontoglossum* was first named in 1815 by Humboldt, Bonpland, and Knuth, using the Greek words *odonto* (tooth) and *glossa* (tongue), a reference to the toothlike projections on the lip. *Brassia* was named in 1813 by R. Brown in honor of William Brass, a botanical illustrator of that era. Both genera hail from tropical and subtropical regions of the New World.

The narrow segments resemble those found in Brassia

Horizontal yellow striping betrays O. grande *in the genetic background*

Odontoglossum
RAWDON JESTER
'HAPPINESS'
This hybrid bears a very strong resemblance to *O. grande* (now named *Rossioglossum grande*).

Odontoglossum praestans
'SAN DAMIANO', HCC/AOS
This Peruvian native's open flower resembles a *Brassia* more than an *Odontoglossum*.

Odontoglossum **MIDNIGHT MIRACLES**
'MICHAEL PALERMO', AM/AOS
The lip color comes from *Odontoglossum* (*Lemboglossum*) *bictoniense*, and the sepal and petal color from *O. cariniferum*.

SEEING SPOTS

Odontoglossum crispum
'SUNSET LACE', AM/AOS
A multitude of outstanding hybrids has been bred from this cool-growing Colombian species. Note the variable spotting.

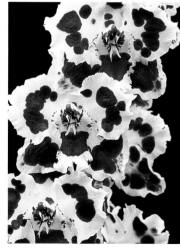

Odontoglossum **TROILUS**
'SNOW LEOPARD'
The overlapping flowers and irregular markings make it difficult to distinguish individual flowers from a distance.

Brassia **SPIDER'S GOLD**
'HILO ORCHID FARM', AM/AOS
Brassia hybrids are undeniably spectacular in full flower: individual flowers can reach up to 14in (35cm) from top to bottom, and a well-grown plant with several bloom spikes easily measures 3ft (1m) across. Some brassias produce a faint vanilla scent.

Brassia CHIEFTAIN 'BIG LOU', JC

ONCIDIUM MULTIGENERICS

Over the years, breeders have crossed many of the genera in the Oncidiinae subtribe, shown on the previous pages, to produce an outstanding array of hybrids with two or more genera in their genetic background. Many have long-lasting, very colorful flowers, neatly arranged on erect to arching spikes. There are six different genera in the genetic makeup of the hybrids shown here.

Odontocidium BIG MAC
This hybrid has the star-shaped flowers and markings typical of *Oncidium* X *Odontoglossum* primary hybrids and is intermediate between the two parents.

Odontioda MOUNT BINGHAM
Often borne on arching sprays, *Odontioda* (*Odontoglossum* X *Cochlioda*) flowers are usually neatly arranged and have the irregular spotting often found in *Odontoglossum* hybrids.

Colmanara WILDCAT 'ALAN J. DAVIDSON', AM/AOS
The popular Wildcat grex, made up of *Miltonia*, *Odontoglossum*, and *Oncidium*, garnered its first flower-quality award in 1975.

Odontorettia RONALD CIESINSKI 'LAGUNA NIGUEL', AM/AOS
The dark vermilion color and flower shape indicate that *Comparettia* is one of the parents (*Odontoglossum* is the other).

Miltassia JUNGLE CAT 'AFRICAN QUEEN', HCC/AOS
The shape, markings, and 4in (10 cm) flower point to *Brassia* in the background of this cross. *Miltonia* is the other parent genus.

Odontioda AVRANCHES 'SAL', AM/AOS
Crystalline white flowers with irregular yellow blotches reveal the role of *Odontoglossum crispum* var. *xanthotes*.

Vuylstekeara LINDA ISLER 'MONTCLAIR', HCC/AO

CATTLEYA ALLIANCE

Encyclia tampensis
'PEGGY', HCC/AOS
First discovered by John Torrey
near Tampa, Florida in 1847, the
Florida butterfly orchid is still
popular, but it is becoming rare
in the wild.

During the first half of the 20th century, some of the most popular of all orchids belonged to the *Cattleya* Alliance; in fact, cattleyas were once proclaimed "Queen of Flowers." Not only have flowers from this group been worn as corsages at countless proms, dances, anniversaries, and weddings, but their images have also adorned china plates, candy boxes, citrus crates, cigar boxes, and even liquor bottles. They are still very popular today, and enthusiastic plant breeders continue to meet the demand for better hybrids. Species of *Cattleya*, *Laelia*, *Sophronitis*, and *Rhyncholaelia* make up the genetic backbone of the hybrids in this group, with *Brassavola*, *Broughtonia*, *Encyclia*, *Epidendrum*, and *Schomburgkia* also playing roles. Other relatives of this alliance include the Pleurothallids (pp. 68-75) and the miscellaneous botanical orchids found on pp. 124-127.

Laelia purpurata var. *werkhauseri*
'KATHLEEN', AM/AOS
This majestic species is one of the most
attractive and popular Brazilian orchids
and is the state flower of Santa Catarina
in Brazil. Also see p. 14.

CATTLEYA SPECIES

Mr. William Cattley, an English horticulturist, saved the first known plants of this genus literally from the trash heap. They had been used as a protective wrapping for some other plants being shipped from South America. When one of the rescuees bloomed, it was recognized as something new to cultivation, and in 1824, Dr. John Lindley named the genus in Cattley's honor.

Cattleya labiata
'GOLIATH', AM/AOS
This is a selection of the first *Cattleya* species tha bloomed in Europe. *Cattleya labiata* has been wide used in breeding and, along with C. *trianaei*, C. *mossiae*, and C. *dowiana* (all shown on these tv pages), is in the genetic background of many of today's outstanding hybrids.

Cattleya mossiae var. *semi-alba*
'CANAIMA'S NIKI',
HCC/AOS
Called the Easter orchid because its bloom season often coincides with Easter.

Cattleya trianaei
'MOOREANA', AM/AOS
If given proper care, this species, which normally blooms only in autumn, can be brought into flower more than once a year.

PROVEN PARENTS

Cattleya aurantiaca
'MARIO PALMIERI DI POLLINA', AM/AOS
Clusters of small, bright orange-red flowers distinguish this species. It has produced some very fine offspring, among them *Cattleya* Chocolate Drop and C. Helene Garcia (both on p. 56).

Cattleya guttata
The unusual color combination has inspired breeders to produce some very attractive hybrids. Crossed with *Cattleya aurantiaca* (left), the resulting seedlings, which first flowered in 1956, were named *Cattleya* Chocolate Drop (p. 56).

GALLERY

tl *Cattleya aclandiae*
'JOE ELMORE', HCC/AOS

tr *Cattleya loddigesii*
'BEAVER VALLEY', AM/AOS

c *Cattleya intermedia* var. *orlata*
'CROWNFOX JEWEL', FCC/AOS

bl *Cattleya dowiana*
'MIDAS TOUCH', AM/AOS

br *Cattleya bicolor*
'DENISE', JC/AOS

CATTLEYA HYBRIDS

It's doubtful that John Dominy of the Veitch Royal Nursery in London realized he was starting a trend when his first *Cattleya* seedling flowered in 1859. He had crossed *Cattleya guttata* (p. 54) with *C. loddigesii* (p. 55), and the result was called *Cattleya* Hybrida. Since then, hundreds of *Cattleya* hybrids have been produced worldwide. With careful selection, even a small greenhouse or basement light setup can have a *Cattleya* hybrid in bloom at any given time throughout the year.

Green segments provide a sharp color contrast with the lip

Cattleya IRIS
The strong influence of *Cattleya bicolor* (p. 55) on this hybrid is especially evident in the lip.

THE OFFSPRING

Cattleya **CHOCOLATE DROP**
'BITTERSWEET', HCC/AOS
Since the grex first flowered in 1965, these attractive offspring of *Cattleya aurantiaca* and *C. guttata* (see p. 54 for both) have been used to create other fine hybrids.

Cattleya **HELENE GARCIA**
The tight flower cluster and the pastel color derive in part from *Cattleya aurantiaca*, one of its parents (see p. 54).

Cattleya **PORTIATA**
'STREETER'S CHOICE', HCC/AOS
More than half of the genes in this grex come from *C. labiata* (p. 54).

The labellum completely encircles the column

Cattleya **BRABANTIAE**
'TRINITY BAY', HCC/AOS
The spots derive from *Cattleya aclandiae*, and the form is from *C. loddigesii* (see p. 55 for both).

Cattleya **PEARL HARBOR**
'ORCHIDGLADE', AM/AOS
The beautiful white-flowered *Cattleya* Bow Bells (registered in 1945) is one parent of this grex.

Cattleya PANACHE AMPHORA 'WALTARI WINE', HCC/AOS

LAELIA SPECIES

It is believed that the pretty, colorful flowers of this genus inspired Dr. John Lindley in 1831 to choose the genus name in honor of either Laelia, one of the Roman vestal virgins, or the female members of the Roman patrician family Laelius. These New World natives range from Mexico to Brazil and are warm to cool growers.

Laelia rubescens
'HEART'S DESIRE', CCM/AOS
The dark coloration in the flower throat distinguishes these delicate flowers. Compare with *L. rubescens* var. *aurea* (below).

Laelia tenebrosa
'VERONICA', AM/AOS
The dark orchid (*tenebrosa* means dark brown) from Brazil is cherished for its unique color combination.

Laelia pumila
'KG'S HOT TICKET',
HCC/AOS
A number of color forms have been attributed to this outstanding dwarf Brazilian species, which is an ideal parent for producing miniature *Laelia* and *Laelia* intergeneric hybrids.

The lip serves as the landing platform for pollinating insects

The pollinia and other reproductive structures are hidden inside the tubular part of the lip

Laelia anceps var. *veitchiana*
Clustered atop long stems, the flowers of this species have been used as decorations for festive occasions in its native Mexico. A number of color forms have been found.

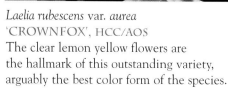

Laelia rubescens var. *aurea*
'CROWNFOX', HCC/AOS
The clear lemon yellow flowers are the hallmark of this outstanding variety, arguably the best color form of the species.

Laelia crispa
The species name refers to the wavy-edged lip. When used as a parent, its open form, recurved petals, and frilled lip tend to dominate the traits of other parents.

Laelia harpophylla 'SONOMA', HCC/AOS

BRASSOLAELIOCATTLEYA AND BRASSOCATTLEYA

The orchid family, unlike many other plant families, readily produces hybrids between two or more genera. In fact, some multigeneric orchid grexes and their hybrids contain genetic material from as many as nine separate genera. The multigeneric hybrids shown here are the results of crossing *Brassavola* (including *Rhyncholaelia*, p. 66), *Laelia* (pp. 58-59), and *Cattleya* (pp. 54-55).

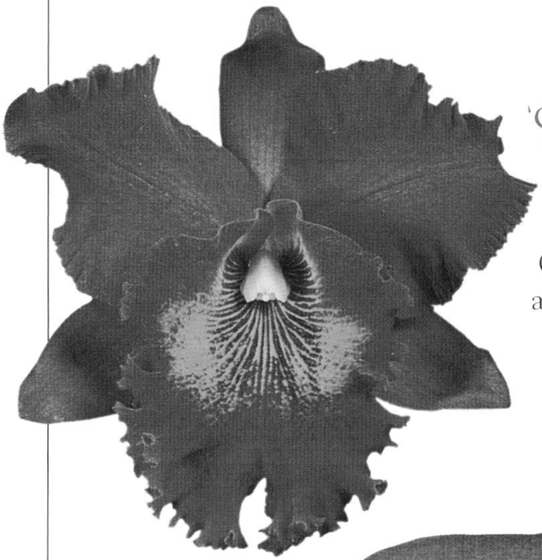

Brassolaeliocattleya NORMAN'S BAY 'GOTHIC', AM/AOS
This large, full flower derives many of its characteristics from *Cattleya labiata* (p. 54) and *C. dowiana* (p. 55).

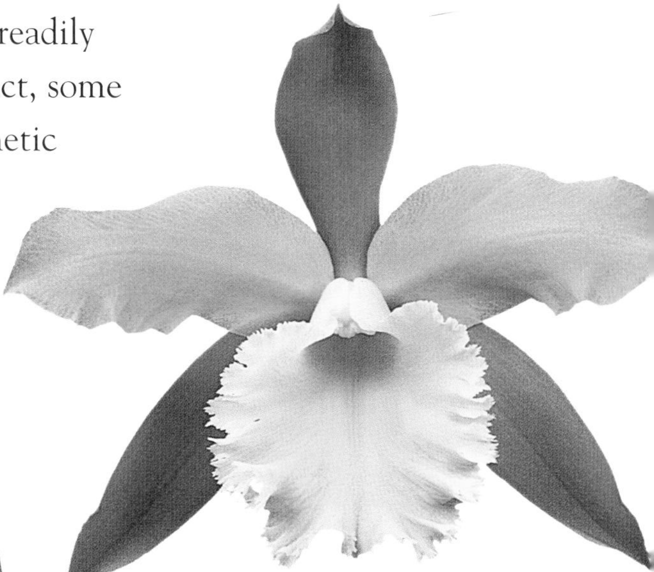

Brassolaeliocattleya LESTER MCDONALD 'MEADOW', HCC/AOS
The wavy, slightly toothed margin on the large lip comes from *Rhyncholaelia digbyana* (p. 66), once included in the genus *Brassavola*.

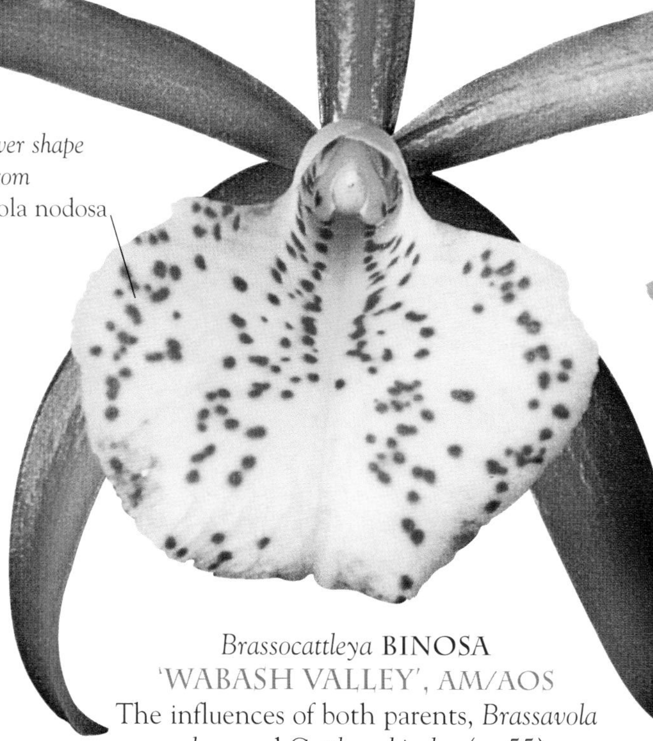
The green segments were inherited from Cattleya bicolor
The flower shape comes from Brassavola nodosa

Brassocattleya BINOSA 'WABASH VALLEY', AM/AOS
The influences of both parents, *Brassavola nodosa* and *Cattleya bicolor* (p. 55), are obvious.

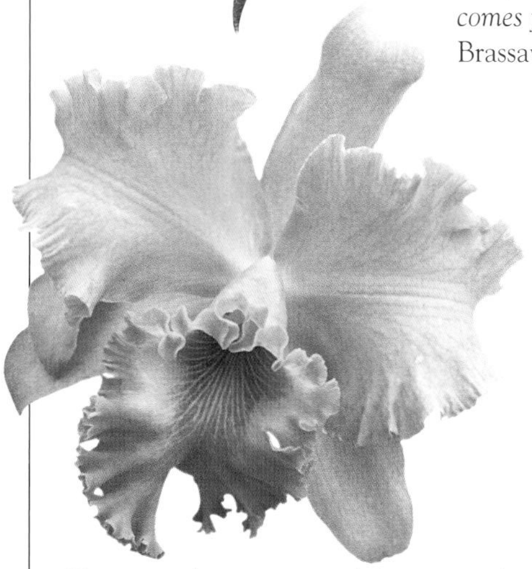

Brassocattleya MOUNT ADAMS
Cattleya mossiae (p. 54) figures prominently in the background of this full flower.

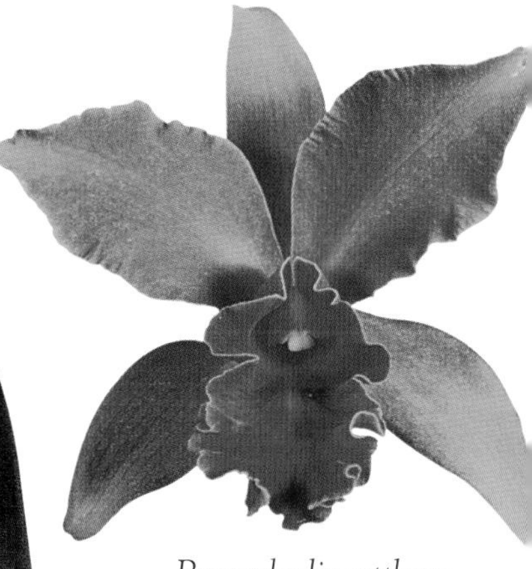

Brassolaeliocattleya GOLDFIELD 'BRONZE PRINCE'
Genes from a variety of species in three different genera occur here.

Brassolaeliocattleya CHYONG GUU CHAFFINCH 'DIXIE'S JOY', HCC/AOS

LAELIOCATTLEYA

The first hybrid in this genus, *Laeliocattleya* Exoniensis, was created by the staff of the Veitch Royal Nursery in London in 1863. It is probably a cross between *Cattleya mossiae* (p. 54) and *Laelia crispa* (p. 58). It's not surprising that hybrids can be made between *Laelia* and *Cattleya*, because there are many genetic similarities between them.

Laeliocattleya
**BURNT ORANGE
'FIREFLY'**
The small, deep yellow flowers of this hybrid show the strong influence of *Cattleya luteola* (*luteola* means "yellow").

Open flowers like this one are called cocktail orchids, after their suitability for corsages

Laeliocattleya
**MEM. ROBERT STRAIT
'BLUE HAWAII', JC/AOS**
The high positioning of the petals is typical of *Cattleya walkeriana* hybrids.

This lip is typical of Cattleya *hybrids of the bifoliate group (they bear two leaves per growth)*

Laeliocattleya
**HARVEST MOON
'RED CHOCOLATE'**
One parent of this grex, *Laeliocattleya* Dormaniana, is of unknown parentage and may descend from *Cattleya bicolor*. There are also two small-flowered laelias in its background.

ORANGE, TOO

Laeliocattleya **TRICK OR TREAT
'ORANGE BEAUTY', HCC/AOS**
The clusters of yellow-orange, open flowers are the result of combining the genes of *Laelia flava*, *Laelia cinnabarina*, and *Cattleya aurantiaca* (p. 54)

Laeliocattleya **ORANGE SHERBET
'ROBBIE', HCC/AOS**
The deep orange color of these flowers can be traced back to one of the grandparents, *Laelia cinnabarina*, whose flowers are vermilion (cinnabar) in color.

GALLERY

tl *Laeliocattleya* **ELIZABETH FULTON**

tr *Laeliocattleya* **ELIZABETH CHANG
'NISHIDA', HCC/AOS**

c *Laeliocattleya* **PIXIE 'CANARY'**

bl *Laeliocattleya* **NIGRESCENT**

br *Laeliocattleya* **COPPER MARK
'COPPER SUMMIT', AM/AOS**

EPIDENDRUM AND ENCYCLIA

Epidendrum, named by Carl von Linne in 1753 from the Greek *epi* (upon) and *dendron* (tree), referring to their habit of growing on trees, includes approximately 500 species that occur naturally from the coastal plain of North Carolina to Brazil. *Encyclia*, named in 1828 by W. J. Hooker from the Greek word *enkylein* (meaning to encircle, referring to the lip around the column in the center of the flower), consists of 150 species ranging from central Florida to Brazil. Most of the species in these two genera require warm to intermediate temperatures to grow well in cultivation.

Epidendrum **TROPICAL BEES** 'FEUERBACH', AM/AOS
Up to 100 of these flowers swarm in clusters on stems to 64in (1.6m) long.

The sepals and petals resemble those of Encyclia tampensis *(p. 53), while the lip is from its other parent,* Encyclia cordigera *(see left)*

Encyclia cordigera 'MAURICE', HCC/AOS
Enthusiasts prize the unusual color combination of the rich chocolate-brown sepals and petals and the rose-purple lip of this Central American native. As a bonus, the flowers are long-lasting.

The column is almost hidden by the encircling lip

Epidendrum **ATROPINE** 'FANGTASTIC', HCC/AOS
Registered in 1962 as an *Epidendrum*, its parents are now both classed as *Encyclia*.

REED-TYPE SPECIES

Epidendrum **HOKULEA** 'PALMER ORCHIDS', CCM/AOS
The inset shows grexmate *Epi.* Hokulea 'Firestorm', AM/AOS.

Epidendrum pseudepidendrum 'YASNA', AM/AOS
The waxy sheen and tubular red lip are two hallmarks of a hummingbird-pollinated flower.

Epidendrum ilense 'LIL', HCC/AOS
Long, arching to pendent stems bear a small cluster of flowers at their tips. Native to Ecuador.

Encyclia cochleata 'DANCING LADY', HCC/AOS
The clamshell orchid is the first tropical American orchid brought into bloom in Europe.

Epidendrum (Nanodes) medusae

OTHER GENERA

Great floral diversity is one of the many attributes that has made the *Cattleya* Alliance an important part of the orchid family, and this is especially evident in the modern hybrids shown on previous pages. The genera depicted on these two pages show some of the other naturally occurring members of the Alliance as well as two manmade genera, *Epilaeliocattleya* and *Diacattleya* (see below). To view some multigeneric hybrids made with genera on this page, see *Brassolaeliocattleya* Lester McDonald (p. 60) and the *Sophrolaeliocattleya* grex on p. 15.

Sophronitis coccinea
'MERILEE', AM/AOS
This modest-sized species from eastern Brazil is a very desirable parent, transmitting its bright coloration to its offspring.

The species is native to only a limited part of southwest Colombia and northwest Ecuador

Broughtonia sanguinea
This native of Jamaica and Cuba has been used to produce small, brightly colored, multiflowered hybrids.

Schomburgkia splendida
'ROBERTO', AM/AOS
The flower shown here is typical of the genus, which usually bears its flowers in clusters atop stiff, erect stems that can be more than 5ft (1.5m) tall.

FRINGE

Rhyncholaelia digbyana
'DRAGONSTONE', CCM/AOS
Formerly classified as a *Brassavola*, this species is in the background of hundreds of hybrids that can readily be recognized by their large, fringed lips.

INTERGENERIC HYBRIDS

Epilaeliocattleya KENNETH ROBERTS
'BOON', HCC/AOS
The size and shape of the flower are an inheritance from *Encyclia tampensis* (p. 53), and the labellum color comes from *Epilaeliocattleya* Carolyn Contorno.

Diacattleya CHANTILLY LACE
'BUTTONS & BOWS'
The unusual petal markings are typical of a semipeloric flower, in which the petals resemble the labellum. Semipeloric and peloric orchids are increasing in popularity.

PLEUROTHALLIDS

This group, encompassing approximately 28 tropical American genera, contains more than 3,000 species. The vast majority of the species are small to miniature plants bearing, in many cases, very small flowers. In a number of genera, the enlarged sepals are the dominant floral segments (see *Masdevallia*, pp. 70-71), with the petals and lip being small to minute. The petals are sometimes reduced to almost hairlike structures. Pleurothallid flowers are very diverse, almost defying anyone to write a general floral description for the alliance. Many of these genera so closely resemble one another, especially vegetatively, that it is difficult even for taxonomists to sort and classify them, even when in flower. The Pleurothallids, all sympodial epiphytes, are warm to cool growers. Many thrive and flower when they are grown in closed cases with controlled humidity and temperature, such as a Wardian case or terrarium.

Lepanthes zamorensis
'FREE SPIRIT', CBR/AOS
It normally takes a magnifying lens to see the charm and beauty of this petite flower.

Masdevallia deformis
'PERFECTO', HCC/AOS
The tube of joined sepals hides the two minute petals and very small lip.

MASDEVALLIA

This genus, first described in 1794 by Ruíz and Pavón, is named in honor of José Masdevall, a 16th-century botanist. Note the long, attenuated appendages (caudae) at the tip of the sepals, which are fused at their base to form a sepaline tube. The tube often completely hides the tiny petals and the very small lips on these flowers, giving the impression that the flowers are composed of only three sepals. Mostly cool growers, masdevallias occur naturally from Mexico south to Brazil and Bolivia.

Masdevallia **TANAGER**
'TRADER'S POINT', HCC/AOS
The broad opening in the sepaline tube in this flower reveals the column and two small petals.

This species has a unique set of lateral sepals

Masdevallia **CHARISMA**
'KEENO'
Bold stripes enhance the simple, sculpted beauty of this broad-sepaled flower.

The petals, lip, and column are hidden in this tube

Masdevallia triangularis **'ALPHA'**
Disregarding the caudae, the broad basal portions of the sepals form an almost perfect equilateral triangle, hence the species name.

Caudae vary in length, even on a single flower

The caudae on the lateral sepals often cross

Masdevallia **FALCON SUNRISE**
The intense flower color (from the red form of M. *coccinea* or the deep orange-red M. *ignea*) is typical of many modern *Masdevallia* hybrids.

Masdevallia **PIXIE LEOPARD**
'WILLIAMSBURG'S JEF',
AM/AOS
This typical *Masdevallia* flower echoes the irregular spotting found on leopards, hence the grex name.

Masdevallia **PIXIE LAVENDER**

OTHER PLEUROTHALLIDS I

The genera depicted on these two pages are typical examples of some of the great variety found among the interesting and unusual flowers of this alliance. Some have caudae (tails, as in *Dracula*), while others do not (*Pleurothallis*). In many cases, the two petals are reduced to almost hairlike structures (*Restrepia*). The floral structure of some *Dracula* species looks like miniature monkeys staring at you (see the photo at far right), while others are less facelike (as in the related *Dracuvallia* Blue Boy to the right).

Both parents have prominent caudae ("tails")

Restrepia sanguinea 'WALTER'
Like many members of this alliance, in this genus the predominant, showy parts of the flowers are the sepals. The species name alludes to the blood red flowers.

Dracula sodiroi
This species' orange color is unique in the genus *Dracula*. Also, here is one of the few draculas that bear more than one flower per inflorescence.

Dracuvallia BLUE BOY NO. 2
Hybrids between *Dracula* and *Masdevallia* often combine the interesting features of both: a facelike pattern and strong coloration.

PLEUROTHALLIS

Pleurothallis hamosa 'D & B', CHM/AOS
The arrangement of the flower stem and flowers lightly resting on the leaf blade occurs in a number of species in this genus.

Pleurothallis paquishae 'TRADERS POINT', CBR/AOS
A cross-shaped arrangement of the floral parts is typical of many in this genus. Note how the flower appears to sit on the leaf.

Pleurothallis niveoglobula
The specific name very neatly describes this dainty white (*nive*) globe (*globus*). Each flower is barely .1in (3mm) across, no larger than some raindrops.

Pleurothallis dunstervillei 'HOOSIER', CBR/AOS
All of these flowers arise from the point where the leaf is attached to the small stem. A number of species flower this way.

OTHER PLEUROTHALLIDS II

An abundance of interesting and extraordinary flowers occurs in the Pleurothallid Alliance. Many of the flowers are so small they must be viewed through a hand lens to enjoy their true beauty, and the plants themselves are often not much bigger (for an extreme example, see *Platystele minimiflora*, below). In nature, there are often many plants of the same species growing side by side; for what they lack in size, they make up for in sheer numbers. These are warm to cool growers, often found naturally in areas of high relative humidity.

Oddly lipped flowers borne singly are two traits of this genus

Barbosella australis (cucullata)
These flowers, arising from the junction between the leaf and the stem, are held well above the leaf blade.

Platystele minimiflora
This tropical Central and South American native is truly miniature: the rice grain at the lower right gives a clear idea of the scale.

Trisetella hoeijeri
The generic name refers to the almost hairlike tips of the sepals on these tropical Central and South American natives. The flowers measure 1.5in (4cm) across.

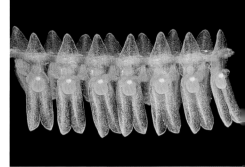

Lepanthopsis floripectin
The flowers, aligned neatly in two rows along the stem, make the inflorescence look like a miniature comb. Of note are the very thin (almost translucent) floral segments.

— LEPANTHES —

Lepanthes lindleyana
This miniature can be found growing in the wild from Costa Rica south to Venezuela. The lip may look large in the picture, but it measures only .04 x .1in (1 x 2mm)!

Lepanthes felis
A native of Colombia, this has flowers almost 0.6in (1.5 cm) in diameter, with two dark green petals that some say resemble eyes, perhaps like those of a cat (*felis* in Latin).

Lepanthes calodictyon
'EICHENFELS', CHM/AOS
The small 1.5in (4cm) leaves are some of the most attractive in the orchid family and beautifully complement the flowers.

Lepanthes medusa 'SHANDOAH'S PIPER', CBR/AO

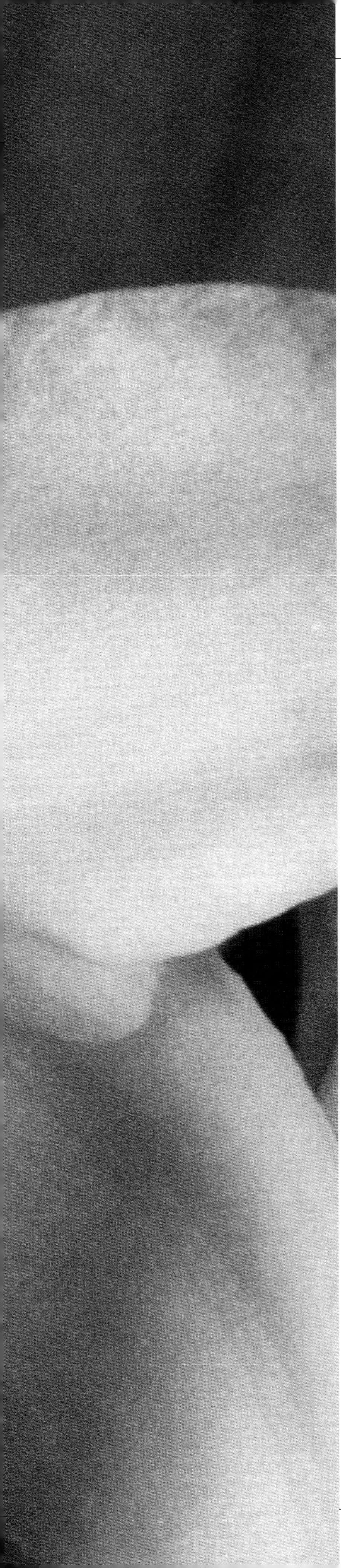

DENDROBIUM

Of all the genera in the orchid family, *Dendrobium* is probably the most diverse. It covers almost the entire western half of the Pacific Ocean basin from the snow line on Mt. Fuji, Japan, as far south as New Zealand and from the islands in the western Pacific all the way west to India. As a result of the great diversity, there are between 900 and 1,400 species in this genus, depending on the taxonomic authority you choose to follow. Plants range from about 2in (5cm) high (*Dendrobium tixieri*) to robust plants with canes 8ft (2.4m) long (*Dendrobium superbum*). Flower longevity ranges from species whose flowers live for one day (*Dendrobium crumenatum*) to those whose individual flowers remain open for eight to ten months (*Dendrobium cuthbertsonii*, see p. 80), a feat unsurpassed by any other species in the plant kingdom. Widely grown in Hawaii and southeast Asia, *Dendrobium* has been the backbone of the orchid cut-flower business for many years.

Dendrobium harveyanum
It's unusual for the petals of an orchid flower to be more heavily fringed than the lip.

Dendrobium **MOUNT FUJI**
This flower is a typical example of the *Dendrobium nobile* group (p. 80).

DENDROBIUM SPECIES I

This genus was first described in 1799 by Olaf Swartz, who coined the generic name from the Greek words *dendron* (tree) and *bios* (life), based on the epiphytic nature of these plants growing on trees. They range from cool (*Dendrobium nobile*, p. 80) to warm growers (*Dendrobium phalaenopsis* hybrids, p. 82). In cultivation, many dendrobiums thrive when confined to small pots.

The flowers in this cluster are just starting to open

The contorted floral segments are the hallmark of this species

Dendrobium densiflorum
This fall-blooming species is similar to *D. thyrsiflorum* (see right) in flower, but it bears yellow-orange blooms.

Dendrobium unicum
The species name means "unique," which is an apt reference to the unusual flower shape of this native of Thailand.

Dendrobium thyrsiflorum
This beauty from Nepal bears its spectacular, massive, pendent heads of colorful flowers in spring. Unfortunately, its flowers remain open for only a few days.

Dendrobium cucumerinum
The odd-looking leaves clearly suggested the specific name for this Australian native: they look like little cucumbers (the Latin name for cucumber is *cucumeris*). Equally odd, the graceful, inverted flowers provide a measure of added interest.

Dendrobium speciosum var. *hillii*
'EL QUESO GRANDE', CCM/AOS
The Australian rock lily can be spectacular when grown attached to a large boulder situated out in the full sun. The plant shown here is extremely well grown, earning the grower a CCM award (see p. 150).

Dendrobium chrysotoxum
'SUSANNE', CCM/AOS
The waxy-textured flowers of this native of Thailand are presented on arching to pendent, airy clusters, thus displaying each flower to its best advantage. *Chrysotoxum* refers to the golden flowers.

Dendrobium bullenianum (topaziacum

DENDROBIUM SPECIES II

These two pages and the previous two pages present only a small sample of the diversity of flower forms found within *Dendrobium* (taxonomists have, over the years, divided this genus into as many as 41 different sections). Likewise, their flower colors encompass virtually the entire floral spectrum, with the exception of true blue (although there are some bluish lavender examples).

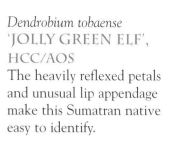

Dendrobium tobaense
'JOLLY GREEN ELF',
HCC/AOS
The heavily reflexed petals and unusual lip appendage make this Sumatran native easy to identify.

Odd lip feature

Sometimes the flowers of this species are green, but they are always edged in brown

Dendrobium tetragonum
This species, which grows naturally only in Australia, not only has an unusual flower but also has odd, rectangular pseudobulbs (see its offspring *Dendrobium* Star of Gold on p. 85).

Dendrobium laevifolium
'MARCELLA', AM/AOS
Native to the islands around Guadalcanal, this grows primarily in moss on the ground or on heavily mossed branches. Sometimes the flowers are hidden by the moss.

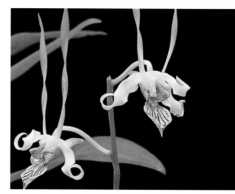

Dendrobium antennatum var. *d'albertisii*
The species name is a reference to the two erect, twisted, antenna-like petals. Dendrobiums with twisted petals are sometimes referred to as "antelope-type." Compare with *D. spectabile* (below).

Dendrobium nobile
This southeastern Asian species has been widely grown and used in hybridizing for its characteristic of producing two or three flowers at every node on the stem. Well-grown plants bear up to 200 flowers per stem.

Dendrobium spectabile
Hailing from New Guinea and the nearby islands, *Dendrobium spectabile* truly is a spectacle when displaying its grotesquely shaped flowers. Plants need to be very large and potbound in order to bloom.

Dendrobium cuthbertsonii
'BLAZE', AM/AOS
When well grown and covered with flowers, these miniature plants become a ball of color. Flowers occur in a range of shades of red, pink, orange, yellow, and purple.

Dendrobium smillieae

DENDROBIUM HYBRIDS I

In 1855, the Veitch Royal Nursery in London registered their first hybrid, *Dendrobium* Dominianum, a cross of *D. linawianum* and *D. nobile* (see p. 80). Although not as plentiful as in other genera (for example, *Phalaenopsis* and *Paphiopedilum*), *Dendrobium* hybrids have come a long way in the past 150 years. Today, interest in *Dendrobium* breeding centres around cut-flower and compact potted-plant types for the florist industry, especially in Hawaii.

The lip c⟨ echoes th⟩ pattern o⟨ the sepal⟨ and peta⟨

Dendrobium KING DRAGON 'MONTCLAIR', HCC/AOS
This *Dendrobium phalaenopsis* hybrid typical of the cut-flower types, has ⟨ shelf life of up to three weeks.

Dendrobium
KURANDA CLASSIC
'QUICK', AM/AOS
Petal-peloric flowers, wherein the lip is similar to the petals and the flower is extremely flat, are becoming popular.

The lip is virtually indistinguishable from the two petals

Dendrobium YUKIDARUMA 'KING', AM/AOS
Bred for the potted-plant trade, this hybrid from 1973 bears up to three flowers per leaf axil (where the leaf joins the stem).

A contrasting color is usually present on the lip

See p. 76 for another hybrid of Dendrobium nobile

Dendrobium MALONES 'HOPE'
Dendrobium nobile hybrids, which have their entire stems covered with flowers, come in many color forms.

Dendrobium
PALE DOREEN 'GUO LUEN', HCC/AOS
The strong contras⟨ between the pale sepals and much darker petals and lip add to the appeal of this *D. phalaenopsis* hybrid.

Dendrobium **ROY YAHIRO** 'ORCHID ACRES STEPHANIE', HCC/AO⟨

DENDROBIUM HYBRIDS II

Diversity increases the more you explore the hybrids within this genus. Yet even with all the hybrids available today, the potential for newer, even more interesting hybrids is almost unlimited, especially for compact potted plants. Conveniently, *Dendrobium* seedlings often flower earlier than those of many other popular genera, allowing for more rapid breeding progression with this genus.

Dendrobium KIRSCH 'LADY HAMILTON'
Dating to 1953, this D. phalaenopsis hybrid has produced many progeny.

Neatly arranged flowers are preferred by growers because they are potentially more awardable

Twisted floral segments occur in a number of Dendrobium species and hybrids

Dendrobium
DOCTOR POYCK 'RYAN'S GRAND SLAM', AM/AOS
Full, neatly arranged, richly colored flowers earned the Award of Merit for this hybrid.

Dendrobium
TOUCH OF GOLD 'T.J.', HCC/AOS
Crossing *Dendrobium gouldii* and *D. johannis* produced open flowers with twisted floral segments.

Dendrobium CRYSTAL PINK 'RHON-RON', HCC/AOS
This recent hybrid (1996) makes a dramatic pot plant, with flowers cascading down the entire stem. Ideally, the flowers bloom simultaneously.

Dendrobium
JESMOND TREASURE 'SPIDER'
The flower's shape, color pattern, and lip leave no doubt that *Dendrobium tetragonum* (p. 80) is one of the parents of this hybrid.

Dendrobium HALEAHI STRIPES 'CHI', JC/AOS
Uniform and unusual striping on the flowers was recognized by American Orchid Society judges, who awarded this hybrid a JC (see p. 150).

DENDROBIUM
SUMMER SUNRISE
Flowers appear at the apex of both the new and old growths of this compact hybrid of *Dendrobium bullenianum* (p. 79) and *Dendrobium lawesii*.

Dendrobium STAR OF GOLD

VANDA ALLIANCE

Christieara
CROWNFOX MAGIC LANTERN
This colorful, round, flat flower is
typical of better modern hybrids.

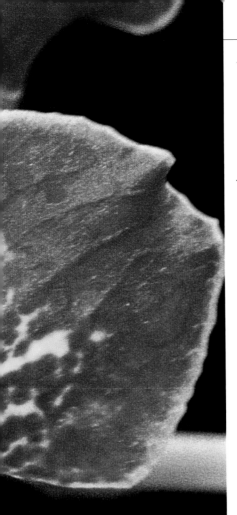

The more than 100 genera and 2,000 species included in the *Vanda* Alliance occur most abundantly in southeastern Asia, tropical Africa, and Madagascar.

Monopodial (upright, fanlike) growth and lack of the swollen pseudobulbs found at the base of many other orchids are characteristics of many in this group, but wide differences occur in plant size, flower size, and number of flowers per inflorescence. Since World War II, the popularity of vandaceous orchids has increased dramatically, especially in tropical and subtropical regions, including Florida, and recently hybridizers have been making many new multigeneric crosses (pp. 96-97). Most are warm growers and can be grown in a slatted basket with little or no medium. For other relatives of this alliance, see the *Phalaenopsis* Alliance (pp. 98-109) and the miscellaneous botanical orchids presented on pp. 132-137.

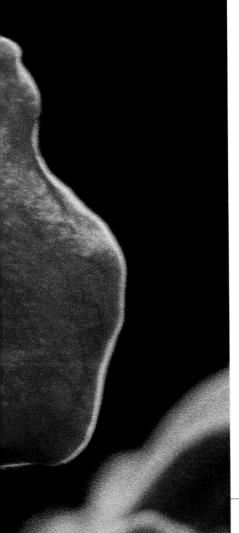

Ascocenda **MOTES HOT CHESTNUT**
'TONY BETANCOURT', HCC/AOS
The color and pattern on this open-faced flower
reflect the influence of *Vanda merrillii*, a parent.

VANDA SPECIES

Sir William Jones was the first to identify *Vanda* as a genus, describing *Vanda roxburghii* in 1795. He adopted the Sanskrit word *vanda*, used by the locals to describe some parasitic plants (it was once believed that epiphytic plants such as vandas were parasitic, taking their nutrition from living plants). This genus grows naturally in the Old World tropics from the Philippines to eastern India, and they are prized greenhouse subjects around the world.

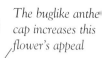

The buglike anther cap increases this flower's appeal

Vanda coerulescens
The specific name indicates that the flowers have a bluish cast. Native to Thailand and Myanmar (formerly Burma).

Vanda tricolor
'VIVA BOTANICA',
HCC/AOS
This species, found mainly in Java and Bali, is a robust grower and often flowers three times a year. Widely used in hybridizing, it passes along its open, colorful flowers to its offspring (see the two selections of *Vanda* First and Last on pp. 90-91).

——YELLOW, TOO——

Vanda denisoniana
Named in honor of Lady Denison Londesbrough, who was a 19th-century orchid enthusiast. The clear yellow flowers make this species a popular choice among today's orchidophiles as well.

Vanda (Euanthe) sanderiana
'CHRIS', FCC/AOS
The orchid known as Wailing-waling to natives of the Philippines has probably been the most important parent in *Vanda* hybridization.

——THE ROTHSCHILD FAMILY——

Vanda **ROTHSCHILDIANA**
This hybrid resulted from the mating of *Vanda (Euanthe) sanderiana* and *Vanda coerulea*. It has been widely used as a parent since 1931 to produce flat, full, round-flowered hybrids.

Vanda coerulea 'EVELYN',
FCC/AOS
The flat, checkered flowers occur in an even bluer form. Native to India eastward to Thailand, *V. coerulea* has been widely used in the quest for true blue.

Vanda tricolor 'SUMMERLAND', HCC/AOS

VANDA HYBRIDS

The first hybrid *Vanda*, officially registered in 1893, was a cross between two terete-leaved (pencil-like) vandas, *Vanda hookeriana* and *Vanda teres*. It was named *Vanda* (*Papilionanthe*) Miss Joaquim in honor of the woman in whose Singapore garden it was discovered. Some 50 years later it became the main flower used in leis, the Hawaiian flower garlands. Today, many hybridizers are striving to develop flat, round flowers in a wide range of colors.

Vanda **MOTES BUTTERCUP** 'DENISE', AM/AOS
The flower color and lip shape indicate that *Vanda denisoniana* (p. 88) is one parent, but the flower is much fuller.

Vanda **CROWNFOX PINK GLOW** 'MARIE DAGUIA', AM/AOS
The genes derived from *Vanda* (*Euanthe*) *sanderiana* (p. 88) are evident in this flower's shape and coloration.

Vanda **FIRST AND LAST** 'GLADYS BERRIOS', AM/AOS
This open-type flower is typical of the offspring arising from *Vanda tricolor* (p. 88).

Vanda **ROSE DAVIS** 'CROWNFOX SNOW', JC/AOS
Crossing *Vanda* Rothschildiana back onto *Vanda coerulea* (see p. 88 for both parents) produced this delightful, pale lavender-blue flower.

─────── BRIGHT AND AIRY ───────

─── FULL AND ROUND ───

Vanda **BILL BURKE** 'REDLAND FESTIVAL', CCM/AOS
The color of the sepals and petals traces back to the *Vanda denisoniana* parent (p. 88), and the lip is from *Vanda cristata*.

Vanda **STAR ELITE** 'MEMORIA VERN ANDERSON', AM/AOS
This flower's lip reflects *Vanda cristata* in its background, while the pale color is inherited from *Vanda coerulescens* (p. 88).

Vanda **GORDON DILLON** 'MEMORIA KHOI TRUONG', AM/AOS
Full, round flowers in a variety of colors are the hallmarks of this grex. Some grexmates have almost blue flowers.

OTHER VANDACEOUS GENERA

In addition to *Vanda*, there are many interesting and colorful genera in the vandaceous section of the orchid family. These southeastern Asian natives, all monopodial epiphytes and warm growers, often produce large numbers of flowers on sprays up to 3ft (1m) long. Many of the other vandaceous genera have been hybridized with *Vanda* to produce some outstanding multigeneric hybrids (pp. 94-95).

Renanthera storiei
The huge sprays of flowers arising from both sides of a stem make this plant a flower show in itself.

Renanthera imschootiana
Broad, leaflike appendages are part of the lateral (side) sepals.

Aerides flabellatum
These plants are exceptionally showy when in flower, with a number of arching inflorescences often in bloom at the same time.

Rhynchostylis retusa
The long, pendent, densely flowered inflorescences of this tropical Asian species inspired the evocative common name of foxtail orchid.

Renanthera monachica
The individual, long-lasting flowers (one of the smaller examples in the genus) of this native of the Philippines stand out on the airy flower cluster.

Ascocentrum miniatum
This yellow color variant of a popular miniature from southeastern Asia has been used widely to breed *Ascocenda* hybrids (pp. 94-95).

Ascocentrum miniatum
Like the yellow variant shown on the left, orange-flowered examples of this species have been widely used in breeding. Also known as *A. garayi*.

Ascocentrum ampullaceum 'AIDA CRUZ', CCM/AOS

ASCOCENDA

Dr. C. P. Sideris registered the first *Ascocenda*, Portia Doolittle, in 1949. However, it was the second offering, *Ascocenda* Meda Arnold, registered in 1950, that began a trend that has since produced a succession of very showy and colorful hybrids. Since its introduction, A. Meda Arnold has garnered more than 60 American Orchid Society flower-quality awards and has produced many offspring. The happy marriage between *Ascocentrum* and *Vanda* has become a major boon to the orchid world.

Ascocenda **THAI FRIENDSHIP** 'MARY MOTES', AM/AOS
Flowers with solid colors and light tessellation (checkering) are very popular but are rarer than their spotted cousins.

The labellum is the smallest part of the Ascocenda flower, but it still plays a part in its overall appeal

Ascocenda **PAKI LONG** 'REDLAND SUNSPOTS', HCC/AOS
Although this flower received a flower-quality award (HCC), it would have received a higher award (AM) had the floral segments been broader and nearly overlapped.

Ascocenda **SUKSAMRAN SPOTS** 'SUNI', AM/AOS
This is a fine example of the full, round, colorful flowers hybridizers work to create.

The golden labellum contrasts nicely with the red-violet floral segments

Ascocenda **NATALIE MAJEWSKI** 'NORMA', AM/AOS
The buttery yellow color with varying degrees of reddish spotting typifies many of today's *Ascocenda* hybrids.

Ascocenda **YIP SUM WAH** 'TOMATO', AM/AOS
This excellent, dark crimson, full flower shows why this grex has received more than 100 flower-quality awards and is so popular as a breeding parent.

Ascocenda **CROWNFOX GOLDEN DAWN** 'MIRAMAR', AM/AOS

VANDACEOUS MULTIGENERICS

There are many manmade hybrid genera in the *Vanda* Alliance that have produced an outstanding array of grexes and selections from them. Note: when the genus name ends in *-ara*, such as in *Christieara* or *Mokara*, at least three distinct genera comprise it.

Uniformity of spots is a breeding goal

Spots are larger and darker on the lower sepals

Renanthopsis
MILDRED JAMESON
A *Renanthera* was mated with a *Phalaenopsis* (a genus within the *Vanda* Alliance but usually considered a separate horticultural group) to produce this bigeneric cross.

Mokara **REDLAND SUNSET**
'ROBERT', AM/AOS
Here is the union of the genera *Arachnis*, *Ascocentrum*, and *Vanda*.

Christieara **MICHAEL TIBBS**
'REDLAND', FCC/AOS
This full, round flower is the result of combining the genes of *Aerides*, *Ascocentrum*, and *Vanda*.

VASCOSTYLIS

Vascostylis **PRECIOUS**
'GRETA VON KRONE', HCC/AOS
An erect spike of well-presented flowers is typical of this trigeneric genus.

Vascostylis **CYNTHIA ALONSO**
'REDLAND', HCC/AOS
The union of *Ascocentrum*, *Rhynchostylis*, and *Vanda* made this grex, whose flower shape recalls *Ascocentrum*.

Vascostylis **BONBON**
'FUCHS INDIGO', AM/AOS
To date, this grex has come closest to producing clear blue flowers, something not often found among orchids.

GALLERY

tl *Christieara* **FUCHS CONFETTI**
'ROBERT', HCC/AOS

tc *Perreiraara* **CROWNFOX AGATE**
'BUTTER BABY', AM/AOS

tr *Kagawara* **CHRISTIE LOWE**
'REDLAND', HCC/AOS

cl *Christieara* **RENEE GERBER**
'FUCHS SPOTTY', AM/AOS

c *Mokara* **MICHAEL CORONADO**
'FUCHS SPOTS', AM/AOS

cr *Vascostylis* **CROWNFOX MAGIC**

bl *Aeridovanda* **FUCHS JEWELL**
'ROBERT', AM/AOS

bc *Aeridovanda* **ARNOLD SANCHEZ**
'BUTTERBALL', HCC/AOS

br *Aeridovanda* **BARNEY GARRISON**
'AILEEN', AM/AOS

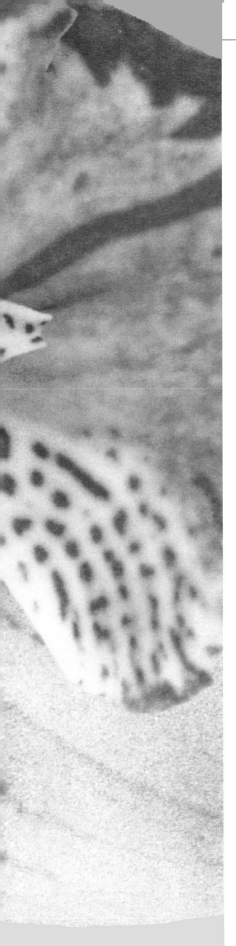

PHALAENOPSIS ALLIANCE

Doritaenopsis
SOGO MARIA
'ORIENTAL STRIPES', HCC/AOS
Fullness of flower and uniformity of
the reddish purple stripes make this a
desirable hybrid.

T he genera treated in this section (*Phalaenopsis* and *Doritis*, as well as *Doritaenopsis*, the hybrid genus made between them) encountered a phenomenal surge in popularity during the last few decades of the 20th century, and currently they rank among the most popular of all flowering potted plants. Approximately 50 species compose *Phalaenopsis*, an Old World genus of tropical monopodial species ranging naturally from Taiwan south to Australia and from the Philippines west to the islands in the Indian Ocean. The flowers are generally remarkably long lived; a spike of *Phalaenopsis amabilis* can have flowers open for several months. A number of species (for example, *Phalaenopsis schilleriana*) have excellent mottled foliage and thus are attractive even when not in flower. The similar-looking and closely related *Doritis* is native to southeastern Asia.

Phalaenopsis SPLISH SPLASH
'PELORIC NO. 3', HCC/AOS
"Triple-lipped" orchids such as this one
are becoming increasingly popular.

PHALAENOPSIS SPECIES I

In 1825, Karl Blume combined the two Greek words *phalaina*, meaning "moth," and *opsis*, a suffix used to indicate similarity to something else, to describe this genus. It is easy to see why he chose the name while inspecting *Phalaenopsis amabilis* (see below): the delicate white flowers with "antennae" on the tip of the lip, neatly arranged on arching spikes and fluttering in the breeze, resemble a cloud of moths settling in for the night.

Phalaenopsis leuddemanniana
This Philippine endemic, which occurs in a number of color forms, has been widely used in hybridization.

Phalaenopsis amabilis
'PAMELA'S PERFECTION',
AM/AOS
The largest-flowered species in the genus, widely distributed from the Philippines to Australia, is the main source of white hybrids.

Phalaenopsis stuartiana
'PETER', HCC/AOS
Attractively marked foliage and large, branched flower clusters, sometimes bearing more than 100 blooms, make this species justifiably popular.

Phalaenopsis parishii
A lovely miniature species, with only a few flowers open at a time. It imparts its unusual lip characteristics to its offspring (see *Phalaenopsis* Mini Mark, p. 106).

Pink has long been a popular Phalaenopsis *color*

Phalaenopsis schilleriana
'AVI', CCM/AOS
This outstanding pink species has been and will continue to be in the background of many choice pink hybrids. Beautifully marked leaves are an added feature.

Phalaenopsis lindenii
Although both the plant and flowers are small, the flowers are produced in generous numbers and open progressively over a long period.

In Phalaenopsis, *the column is often the same color as the floral segments*

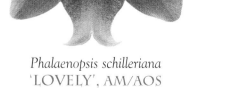

Phalaenopsis schilleriana
'LOVELY', AM/AOS
Like its relative 'Avi' (see left), 'Lovely' is a fine selection of a popular species.

PHALAENOPSIS SPECIES II

During the first half of the last century, white and pink *Phalaenopsis* (as pictured on pp. 100-101) were the dominant species grown and hybridized. However, they are only a minuscule part of the genus, which contains many interesting and colorful species. Their introduction into the breeding arena has led to a fantastically varied range of hybrids (see pp. 106-107).

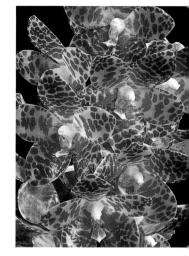

Phalaenopsis gigantea 'MT. VERNON', AM/AOS
The species name is fitting for the largest species in the genus. Its massive, thick leaves have been likened to beaver tails. Unfortunately, the flowers are sometimes hidden beneath or between the leaves and often go undetected.

Not all Phalaenopsis columns are the same color as the floral segments

This toothlike projection is characteristic of the subgenus Polychilos

Phalaenopsis mariae

Phalaenopsis cornu-cervi

Phalaenopsis cornu-cervi, *P. mariae*, and *P. reichenbachiana* all belong to the subgenus *Polychilos*, which is known for its richly colored, nonfragrant, long-lasting flowers that have narrow floral segments. Also, the side lobes of the lip are reduced to toothlike projections (see *P. cornu-cervi* above). Their flowers are produced one at a time along the flowering spike, which can be in bloom for up to a year.

Phalaenopsis reichenbachiana 'ORCHIDPHILE', CBR/AOS

Phalaenopsis equestris 'CANDOR VIOLETTE', FCC/AOS
This diminutive species, with small flowers borne on branched inflorescences, has been used by breeders to produce many multiflora hybrids, some of which have great potential as flowering pot plants.

Phalaenopsis bellina 'HERB'S

PHALAENOPSIS HYBRIDS I

The first *Phalaenopsis* hybrid was registered in 1886 by Veitch Royal Nursery, London. It was a cross between *P. aphrodite* and *P. rosea* (now *P. equestris*; see p. 102) and was named *Phalaenopsis* Intermedia. Over the next 50 years or so the majority of the hybrids produced were white, white with a colored lip, or various shades of pink. During this period, breeders sought to produce larger, rounder, flatter flowers, neatly arranged on gracefully arching sprays.

Phalaenopsis **BROTHER RELAXED FIT** 'ONTARIO LAVA', HCC/AOS
The light orange background color is almost obliterated by the coalescing dark reddish purple spots.

Phalaenopsis **GLAD CHILD** 'YAMAZATO', AM/AOS
This hybrid may have up to 15 neatly arranged flowers open at once.

The pink color appears to be diffusing out from the column

Phalaenopsis **HILO LIP** 'LOVELY'
This grex proved to be a hybridizing breakthrough: before its appearance on the scene, there were no pink *Phalaenopsis* with a white lip.

The amount of color on the base of the lip is highly variable

Phalaenopsis
WILD DELIGHT
'TRAVIS', HCC/AOS
Even though the stripes are not prominent, this hybrid is considered striped.

Phalaenopsis
DAWN TREADER
The pink blush at the base of the floral segments in some members of this grex covers more area, producing an almost pink flower.

Phalaenopsis
MALIBU MINUTE
'LISA', HCC/AOS
The white picotee edge of the floral segments highlights the dark, richly colored veins on these 2in (5cm) flowers. Two rows of neatly arranged flowers were a factor in receiving the HCC award.

PHALAENOPSIS HYBRIDS II

Major changes in *Phalaenopsis* breeding occurred during the last half of the 20th century, when a new array of hybrids appeared. It all began around 1957, when Lewis Vaughn registered the first yellow-flowered hybrid, *P.* Golden Louis. Since then there have been myriad colorful hybrids produced, with new crosses being registered monthly with the Royal Horticultural Society (London).

The lip recalls its parent, P. amboinensis

Phalaenopsis
ZUMA JO
'CHADWICK', HCC/AOS
Richly colored, star-shaped flowers with an enamel-like texture are popular.

Breeders strive to have each flower displayed individually on an inflorescence

Phalaenopsis
EVERSPRING KING
'PANDA', JC/AOS
This is one of an interesting group of recent hybrids. No two flowers have an identical color pattern.

Phalaenopsis **SOGO LION**
'ORCHID WORLD', HCC/AOS
Spots and bars, often in concentric rings, are the hallmark of many newer *Phalaenopsis* hybrids.

Phalaenopsis **MINI MARK**
'SARA MICHELLE', AM/AOS
In a semipeloric flower, the petals look more like the lip than normal petals. The lip comes from its *P. parishii* ancestor (p. 100).

Phalaenopsis
WALDEN'S PUMPKIN PATCH
'ORANGE PASSION', AM/AOS
The orange-red flowers bring another color to *Phalaenopsis* hybrids.

Phalaenopsis **BRECKO DREAMCUP** 'VALLE MIST', HCC/AOS

DORITAENOPSIS AND DORITIS

Doritaenopsis, the result of crossing of *Doritis* and *Phalaenopsis*, contains some very fanciful hybrids. The primary hybrids (crosses between species) tend to have more erect spikes with smaller flowers, many of intense colors. Primary hybrids crossed back on *Phalaenopsis* produce progeny with flowers that look more like *Phalaenopsis*, being fuller, rounder, and borne on more arching sprays (see *Doritaenopsis* Malibu Bay, right).

Doritaenopsis MALIBU BAY 'ZUMA LIPSTICK', AM/AOS
Pristine white flowers with ruby lips are beautifully arranged on an arching spike.

Doritaenopsis BUENA LEMON BRITE 'GOLDEN GLOW', AM/AOS
Yellow flowers, although usually smaller than their pink and white relatives, are much sought after.

Doritaenopsis RED PEARL 'BARBARA ANN', AM/AOS
The flowers obtain their intense red-purple coloration from *Doritis* (below).

DORITIS

Doritis pulcherrima 'A-DORIBIL' HCC/AOS
Over the past two decades, semipeloric forms of this species have been discovered in a variety of colors.

Doritis pulcherrima 'JUNE SNOW' AM/AOS
The white form of *Doritis pulcherrima* is also variable with respect to the amount of yellow on the lip.

Doritis pulcherrima 'FRED JERNIGAN' HCC/AOS
Although flower color is highly variable in this species, this flower shows the more commonly occurring color.

GALLERY

tl *Doritaenopsis* TAISUCO CANDYSTRIPE 'MAJESTIC FLARE', JC/AOS

tr *Doritaenopsis* MALIBU EASTER 'IOSCO BUTTERFLY', JC/AOS

tc *Doritaenopsis* PURPLE GEM 'SNOW COURT', HCC/AOS

cl *Doritaenopsis* MEM. VAL RETTIG 'WALLBRUNN', AM/AOS

cr *Doritaenopsis* MAUI SIZZLE 'MAHALO LOUIE', HCC/AOS

bc *Doritaenopsis* KENNETH SCHUBERT 'ORIENTAL SKY', HCC/AOS

bl *Doritaenopsis* PINATA 'PACIFIC'

br *Doritaenopsis* NUEVO PARAISO 'SQUEAKY', HCC/AOS

BOTANICALS

The term "botanical" is used by orchid enthusiasts to designate any genus or species of orchid that is not grown commercially for its flowers or as flowering potted plants, although many in this group produce showy flowers. The diversity of flower and plant forms within the botanicals is

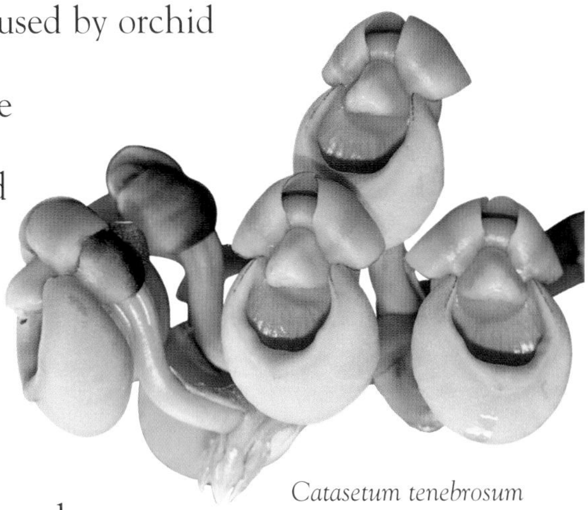

Catasetum tenebrosum 'CLOWN ALLEY', JC/AOS
These flowers are typical of the female blooms found in this genus. The male flowers are more colorful and showy (see p. 116).

immense and could be considered the *magnum opus* of the plant kingdom. This group of genera has been organized in this book according to Dr. Robert Dressler's taxonomic concept of the family (as presented in his book, *Phylogeny and Classification of the Orchid Family*). Here is showcased a small fraction of the interesting and unusual species contained within the confines of this huge family. Their native habitats and cultural requirements span the entire range found within the Orchidaceae. Many of the botanicals shown here are closely related to other genera and alliances presented earlier in this book.

Anguloa ✕rolfei
Flowers of this genus have affectionately been called tulip orchids: at first glance the flowers do resemble tulips.

SPIRANTHOIDEAE AND ORCHIDOIDEAE

The Spiranthoideae subfamily contains what are considered some of the more developmentally primitive members of the family. The related Orchidoideae continues onto the next two pages.

The gland is at the base of the lip

Floral segments are spread like the fingers on a hand

Caladenia catenata
Although it cannot be seen here, the botanical name indicates there is a beautiful (*Cala*) gland (*denia*) attached (*catenata*) to the lip. (Orchidoideae)

The lateral sepals bear long caudae ("tails")

Pterostylis abrupta
There are close to 60 species of *Pterostylis* in Australasia. All have basically green flowers, with varying degrees of striping. At first glance, the flowers resemble Jack-in-the-pulpits (*Arisaema*). (Orchidoideae)

The tip of the lip ("Jack") sticks out

Cryptostylis conspicua
It's all in the name that aptly describes this flower, whose beautiful (*conspicua*) lip hides (*Crypto*) the column (*stylis*). The lips in this genus always encircle the column. (Orchidoideae)

Caladenia dilatata
The thynnid wasp is attempting to mate with the flower. A number of orchid genera rely on pseudocopulation to bring about pollination (see p. 114). (Orchidoideae)

Calochilus robertsonii
The generic name was derived by Robert Brown from the two Latin words *kales* (beautiful) and *cheilos* (lip) to describe the eye-catching hairy lips on these flowers. (Orchidoideae)

Stenorrhynchos speciosum
If mowing is delayed in the spring along several highways in southern Florida, this 2ft (60cm) terrestrial species appears by the thousands in full bloom. (Spiranthoideae)

Pelexia olivacea
'ADANTE', CBR/AOS
The spiral arrangement of the flowers is typical of many Spiranthoideae. The dorsal sepal forms a helmet (*Pelexia*) on these olive-green (*olivacea*) flowers.

Corybas carinatus (Orchidoideae

ORCHIDOIDEAE CONTINUED

This subfamily occurs widely in north temperate Europe (with some members found in Africa, Australia, and South America) and is famous for its various methods of deceit to involve insects in pseudocopulation to bring about the pollination of the flowers (see *Ophrys*, below). Root-stem structures called tuberoids or tubercles are harvested in some parts of the world for use in aphrodisiacs, beverages, and confections.

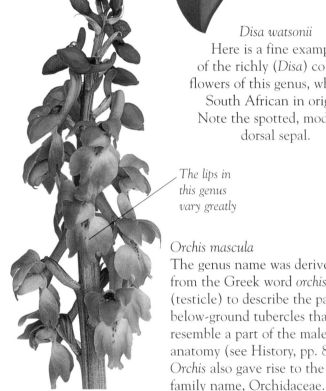

Disa watsonii
Here is a fine example of the richly (*Disa*) colored flowers of this genus, which is South African in origin. Note the spotted, modified dorsal sepal.

DORMANT ORCHIDS

Stenoglottis longifolia
This tropical African species is showy in bloom but goes dormant for almost six months after flowering. The genus name tells us the flower has a narrow (*Steno*) "tongue" (*glottis*).

Habenaria carnea
'ORCHID MAN', CCM/AOS
Like *Stenoglottis* (right), this southeastern Asian is dormant for almost six months, but its colorful foliage and many blooms compensate for that.

The lips in this genus vary greatly

Orchis mascula
The genus name was derived from the Greek word *orchis* (testicle) to describe the pair of below-ground tubercles that resemble a part of the male anatomy (see History, pp. 8-9). *Orchis* also gave rise to the family name, Orchidaceae.

THE MIMICS

The genus *Ophrys* is best known for the mimicry shown by their alluring flowers, whose lips resemble the abdomens of female insects. Male insects, attempting to mate with them, pollinate the flowers, which may also have a scent resembling that of the females.

Apifera *refers to the beelike (apis in Latin) lip*

Ophrys apifera

Ophrys lutea

Ophrys ciliata (vernixia)

Ophrys bornmuelleri

Disa **NOYO 'BLAZE**

CYMBIDIEAE

This tribe is part of the Cymbidiod phylad (pp. 12-13), which derives its name from *Cymbidium* (pp. 34-39). Despite their floral diversity, they are considered a natural group, based on the similarity of their seeds. There are 28 genera in the tribe, distributed worldwide in both tropical and temperate regions. The genera depicted here are sympodial, epiphytic or terrestrial tropical orchids from Africa and the Americas.

Eulophia guineensis
Eulophia is widespread, with members found in Africa, tropical America, the West Indies, and the southern United States. The flowers bloom on erect, upright stems, some up to 3ft (1m) tall.

The labellum is the dominant feature of this flower

CATASETUM

Catasetum species bear separate male and female flowers. The males contain a triggering mechanism that will actually fire the pollinarium (a combination of the pollinia [pp. 10-11] and other structures called the caudicle and the viscidium) at an insect as it enters the flower, usually hitting it near the head. The insect may then pollinate a female flower as it enters it. All the flowers shown here are males, which in this genus are the showy ones. The females are usually green and helmet shaped (see *Catasetum tenebrosum*, p. 111).

Catasetum fimbriatum

Pardalina means "spotted like a leopard"

Cymbidiella pardalina
This native of Madagascar grows in association with a staghorn fern (*Platycerium madagascariense*), which is another epiphyte. The other two species in the genus have entirely different habitats: one grows only on *Rhapis* palms, while the other is terrestrial and grows in living sphagnum moss.

Catsetum barbatum

Catasetum schmidtianum 'CROWN FOX', CHM/AOS

The pure yellow form shown here is less common than spotted variants

Ansellia africana var. *natalensis*
This South African native is so highly variable that taxonomists proposed splitting this species into a number of species, based solely on the colors of the flowers.

Cycnoches **PENTAWAR** 'GAIL', AM/AOS

ZYGOPETALINAE

The 30 genera presently placed in this subtribe within the Cymbidioid phylad show considerable floral variation. Some have one flower per inflorescence, often held close to the base of the plant (*Pescatorea*), while others have erect, multiflowered inflorescences held well above the leaves (*Zygopetalum*). All are sympodial, are either terrestrial or epiphytic, and range from warm to cool growers.

Zygowarrea **SPRINGHURST** 'JIMLOU', AM/AOS
The relatively broad floral segments and flaring lip were inherited from the *Warrea* parent. Upright inflorescences display the flowers above the foliage.

The flat lip completely exposes the column

Cochleanthes **AMAZING** 'DONNAN', AM/AOS
This attractive hybrid received its large lip from its C. *amazonica* parent, which has an extremely large lip.

Zygopetalum **SYD MONKHOUSE** 'EVERGLADES', AM/AOS
Long-lasting, 2.5in (7cm) flowers bloom on erect inflorescences above the leaves.

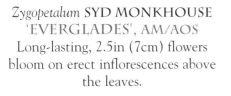

Huntleya flowers are usually star-shaped

Hairs obscure the rest of the lip

Huntleya gustavii 'HATILLO STAR', AM/AOS
Blooms of this tropical American species occur singly on very short inflorescences and open close to the base of the leaves.

Pescatorea lehmannii 'PASSION', AM/AOS
Borne close to the base of the leaves and often hidden among them, this beautiful flower with the very hairy lip may bloom unnoticed.

LYCASTINAE

Many members of this sympodial, tropical American subtribe within the Cymbidiod phylad bear single-flowered inflorescences, but they compensate by producing multiple inflorescences from the base of each pseudobulb (see *Anguloa clowesii* below). They grow at a wide range of elevations in their native habitats, hence they range from cool growers (*Anguloa*) to warm (*Lycaste cruentum*).

Bifrenaria tyranthina
These attractive flowers are borne on very short stems and are sometimes hidden from view by the foliage. Note the strong resemblance to the related *Cymbidium* (pp. 34-39).

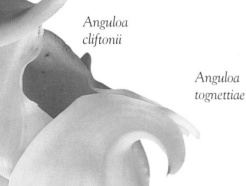

Anguloa cliftonii

Anguloa tognettiae

Anguloa
The South American anguloas are known as the tulip orchids or cradle orchids. Viewed from the side, the flower resembles a tulip (as in *A. cliftonii*). Looking down into the flower from above, with a bit of imagination you can see an infant in a cradle (*A. tognettiae*). Anguloas are very attractive when in full bloom.

GALLERY

tl *Lycaste* **SHOALHAVEN** 'FIRESTORM'

tr *Lycaste aromatica*

tc *Lycaste fulvescens* 'APRICOT JAM', CBR/AOS

cl *Lycaste plana*

cr *Lycaste powellii*

bc *Lycaste fragrans* 'MANZANITA', CHM/AOS

bl *Lycaste locusta*

br *Lycaste* **SUNRAY** 'GUNNER', HCC/AOS

A BIGENERIC HYBRID

Lycaste fulvescens
Not all *Lycaste* flowers are as fully open as shown in the Gallery to the right: some, as seen here, open only partially. Arguably the most interesting aspect of this flower is the heavily fringed lip.

Anguloa clowesii
The most widely known member of the genus produces numerous flowers with lips that rock back and forth. Several single-flowered inflorescences arise from each pseudobulb. Native to the Andes.

Angulocaste **ROSEMARY**
Hybrids between *Anguloa* and *Lycaste* are popular. In many cases, as above, the flowers closely resemble the *Lycaste* parent. All inherit both parents' single flower per inflorescence.

STANHOPEINAE AND MAXILLARIINAE

Both of the subtribes shown here are parts of the Cymbidiod phylad (as also shown on pp. 116-121) One member of the Stanhopeinae, *Peristeria elata*, the dove orchid or Holy Ghost orchid (at right), is the national flower of Panama. The flowers have what appears to be a dove sitting inside each flower.

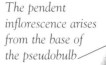

The pendent inflorescence arises from the base of the pseudobulb

Embreea rodigasiana
Like its close relative *Stanhopea*, this must be grown in a basket: the inflorescence grows downward, often through the medium, emerging from the bottom. (Stanhopeinae)

The unusual lip is typical of those found in the Stanhopeinae

Trigonidium egertonianum
The lip, column, and two tiny petals are hidden by the three overlapping, showy sepals. (Maxillariinae)

Mormolyca gracilipes
This cool-growing Andean species bears its flowers singly on tall, thin inflorescences. (Maxillariinae)

─ NO TWO ARE ALIKE ─

Maxillaria fractiflexa
'SONOMA', CHM/AOS
Long, attenuated sepals and curlique petals are found in a number of *Maxillaria* species. (Maxillariinae)

Acineta hennisiana
'SOCRATES', CHM/AOS
Cup-shaped, usually tightly clustered flowers are borne on 30in (1m) long, pendent inflorescences. (Stanhopeinae)

Stanhopea barbata (*costaricensis*)
Stanhopeas are called *El Toro* or *toritos* ("The Bull" or "little bulls"), alluding to the dark spots (eyes) and the hornlike projections on the lip. (Stanhopeinae)

Paphinia cristata
The species name refers to the comblike crest on these New World tropical orchids. Each inflorescence bears one to several flowers. (Stanhopeinae)

Peristeria elata 'WINGED BEAUTY', CCM/AOS (Stanhopeinae)

EPIDENDROID PHYLAD I

The orchids depicted on these two pages belong to two subtribes of this group, the Arethusinae (two temperate Asian and North American genera with fleshy corms) and the Bletiinae (21 genera and several hundred species of mostly pantropical orchids, with a few in temperate Asia and North America). All but *Arethusa* are in the Bletiinae.

Phaius tankervilleae
'RABIN'S RAVEN', AM/AOS
Large clumps put on a spectacular flower show in early spring. For a lighter-colored selection of the nun orchid, see 'Rosita' (right).

Calanthe vestita
From southeastern Asia, this species has been widely used in breeding since 1860 and is still popular with hybridizers today. A number of color forms exist.

Many hybrids have dark spots on the base of the lip beneath the column

Calanthe **VICTORIA KATRINA** 'RED EYE'
The first manmade orchid hybrid (1855) was a cross between two *Calanthe* species. This flower is an example of modern hybrids.

Calopogon tuberosus
The weight of a pollinating insect causes the yellow-bearded lip to flex, bringing the insect in contact with the column below it, helping to ensure pollination.

Tainia hookeriana
Well-grown plants display up to 25 2in (5cm) flowers borne on 3ft (90cm), upright stems. Native to northern Thailand.

Yellow hairs attract pollinating bees

Arethusa bulbosa
The specific name indicates that this is a bulbous (actually cormous) species, a characteristic of the Arethusinae. Commonly called the bog rose.

Phaius tankervilleae 'ROSITA', CCM/AOS

EPIDENDROID
PHYLAD II

Three more subtribes within this phylad, which also includes the *Cattleya* Alliance (pp. 52-67) and the Pleurothallids (pp. 68-75), are presented here. These epiphytic and terrestrial orchids are warm and cool growers.

Coelogyne pandurata
This southeastern Asian sympodial epiphyte bears its 5in (12cm) flowers on 12in (30cm) stems. (Coelogyninae)

For a structural analysis of this flower, see pp. 10-11

The markings and fringe on the lip vary among the 16 known species

---- BIG HYACINTH ----

Arpophyllum giganteum
'SANTA BARBARA', CCE/AOS
The botanic name refers to the stiff, sickle-shaped (*Arpo*) leaves (*phyllum*) on this big (*giganteum*) species. Commonly called the hyacinth orchid. (Arpophyllinae)

Pleione formosana
Showy flowers of this native of China and Taiwan bloom a few inches above ground. (Coelogyninae)

Elleanthus trilobatus
Bracts (leaflike structures at the base of the flowers) are a prominent feature of this genus. Compare this pineconelike inflorescence with the spherical one of E. *sphaerocephala* to the right. (Sobraliinae)

Dendrochilum wenzelii
Unlike others in this southeastern Asian genus, *D. wenzelii* has erect flower spikes. Small flowers appear among the tall, dark green, grasslike leaves. (Coelogyninae)

Coelogyne cristata
Pendent inflorescences bear up to ten 3in (8cm) crystalline white flowers with a distinct yellow lip crest (*cristata* in Latin). (Coelogyninae)

Green bracts contrast with the yellow flowers

Elleanthus sphaerocephala 'EICHENFELS GOOZLE', CBR/AOS (Sobraliinae)

BULBOPHYLLUM I

Bulbophyllums are part of the subtribe Bulbophyllinae in the Dendrobioid Subclade. The genus was first described in 1822 by Thouars, who coined the generic name from two Greek words *bolbos* (bulb) and *phyllon* (leaf). Today there are approximately 1,000 species included in the genus, which now includes all those species formerly known as *Cirrhopetalum*. Many of these tropical Asian plants are quite small, but they produce some remarkable flowers.

Bulbophyllum lemniscatoides 'WAPPINGERS FALLS', CBR/AOS
The species name describes this very well: *lemniscatoides* literally means "looking like an orchid flower with tapes."

Long, attenuated sepals are present on many Bulbophyllum *species*

In most bulbophyllum the lips and petals are minute compared with the sepa[l]

Bulbophyllum lishanensis
Native to Mount Li-shan (*lishanensis*), Taiwan, its flowers are not as neatly arranged as in some other species (compare with *B. makoyanum* on p. 131).

Bulbophyllum **LOUIS SANDER**
The sepals are the first things that catch your eye, but the most attractive portion of the flower is the area around the minute petals and lip, where tiny structures (artifacts) occur.

Bulbophyllum barbigerum
In contrast with many other bulbophyllums, this species has small, nonattenuated sepals, and its major floral segment is a large lip with clavate (club-shaped) hairs at the tip.

Bulbophyllum rothschildianum 'A-DORIBIL', CCM/AOS
The parachute-like arrangement of the flowers makes them appear to be floating around the plant. This well-grown specimen deservedly netted its grower the CCM award.

Bulbophyllum annandalei 'D & B', CHM/AOS
Although the sepals of these flowers are not attenuated, they are still the dominant feature of the flower. The other floral segments are very small and lack the artifacts of their kin, such as *B. barbigerum* (above).

Bulbophyllum binnendijkii 'ODORIFEROUSLY MAGNIFICO', CHM/AOS
The odd name could be applied to a number of *Bulbophyllum* species, such as *B. phalaenopsis*, whose fetid odor makes a lasting impression.

Bulbophyllum medusae

BULBOPHYLLUM II

Diversity within *Bulbophyllum* seems endless. The umbrella-like inflorescences of some are almost daisylike, looking more like single blossoms than the bouquet of flowers they really are. In others, the petals are reduced to almost hairlike structures that wave in the breeze and look like the antennae of an insect emerging from the flower; perhaps the structures attract real insects that might pollinate the flower. Still others are rather plain.

Plain flowers lack artifacts

Bulbophyllum aemulum
'WAPPINGERS FALLS', CHM/AOS
The elongated lateral sepals are tubular and pendent, and the floral parts are unadorned, producing a plain look.

Each "petal" is actually a separate flower

Bulbophyllum wendlandianum
The dorsal (upper) sepal and petals are adorned with varying size hairs that, on the dorsal sepal, appear to be extensions of its linear red stripes.

Bulbophyllum robustum (graveolens)
'CASTLE', AM/AOS
Here is a variation on the theme of daisylike flowers. Compare the unornamented floral parts with the decorated ones to the left.

Bulbophyllum roseopunctatum
'PATRICIA', CHM/AOS
The species name refers to the rose colored dots.

Bulbophyllum frostii
This native of southeastern Asia is typical of some of the plainer, less ornamented flowers found in *Bulbophyllum*. The dovelike interior structure of the small cup-shaped flower is reminiscent of *Peristeria* (p. 123).

Bulbophyllum falcatum var. bufo
Upon first inspection, it looks like this is a member of another genus: the lateral sepals form a tube, and the flowers are devoid of artifacts. Also note how the inflorescence is flattened and the flowers alternate on the stem.

Bulbophyllum auratum
'OTHER WORLD', CHM/AOS
The golden yellow (*auratum*) flowers are more daisylike than many of its kin. Like most daisy types (also see right), the flowers have interesting coloration and markings.

Bulbophyllum makoyanum

AERIDINAE

The Aeridinae is one of the three subtribes of the Vandeae tribe, which in turn is part of the Dendrobioid subclade, which also contains *Dendrobium* (pp. 76-85) and *Bulbophyllum* (pp. 128-131). The largest subtribe in the Vandeae, the Aeridinae contains *Phalaenopsis* and *Doritis* (pp. 98-109) and *Vanda*, as well as a wide variety of botanicals, mostly from tropical Asia, some of which are shown here.

The column is very short and appears to be mostly the anther cap

Floral segments are as thick as a banana peel

Pteroceras appendiculata
The scientific name describes part of this flower very neatly: the lip resembles a winged (*Ptero*) horn (*ceras*) with appendages (*appendiculata*).

Vandopsis gigantea
This robust grower from Myanmar (Burma) looks like a large *Vanda*, with strong, drooping to pendent inflorescences bearing 2.5in (7cm) long-lasting flowers.

Esmeralda clarkei 'BOKAY', CHM/AOS
The two species in this Himalayan genus both bear three to five 2.5-3in (7-8cm) flowers per stem, with *E. clarkei* having the narrower floral segments.

Microsaccus brevifolius
Each flower has a very small (*Micro*) spur (*saccus*) and emerges from the axil of the small (*brevi*) clasping and folded leaves (*folius*). This southeastern Asian native is a warm grower.

Saccolabium kotoense
This small, southeastern Asian native is believed to be related to *Sarcochilus* (right). Although very attractive when in flower, plants are seldom seen in cultivation.

Sarcochilus hartmannii 'ENGLAND'S ROSE', HCC/AOS
As many as 25 densely arranged, attractive, 1.5in (3cm) flowers appear on upright inflorescences. The degree of red spotting varies on this native of Australia.

Aerides crassifolia
The specific epithet refers to the thick, leathery leaves. Short plants bear 5in (12cm) inflorescences with up to ten flowers. Native to Thailand and Myanmar (Burma).

Trichoglottis philippinensis var. brachiata 'VIN-MAR', AM/AOS

ANGRAECINAE

This subtribe contains genera with the largest flowers and the longest spurs (tubular structures at the back of the flower) of any group in the Vandeae. Most of the flowers in this group are white or near white and are pollinated by night-flying hawklike moths. Most come from tropical Africa, Madagascar, and islands in the Indian Ocean.

The dorsal sepal is erect in most Angraecum species

Aeranthes ramosa
The generic name means "air flower": its flower stems are so thin that the flowers appear to be completely dissociated from the rest of the plant.

Aeranthes grandiflora
'SCHNURMACHER',
HCC/AOS
This native of Madagascar bears its flowers at the tips of 20in (50cm), thin, wiry, arching stems.

The lip has a sharp projection at the apex of the midlobe

Angraecum eichlerianum
The spur on this species is unlike that of most of its kin, being very broad at the base of the lip and tapering rapidly to a point, much like a funnel.

Long, thin sepals add to the airy appearance of the flower

Angraecum sesquipedale
'ESTRELLA BLANCA', HCC/AOS
The long-spurred, 12in (30cm) Star-of-Bethlehem orchid from Madagascar blooms in December and has been likened to the star the Magi followed. It is pollinated by a night-flying hawklike moth.

Jumellea arachnanthe
The species name refers to the spidery flowers borne on erect inflorescences that arise from the leaf axils. They are pure white except for the colored column. The genus is native to South Africa, Madagascar, and the islands of the Indian Ocean.

Oeonia volucris
Known only from Madagascar and the Mascarene Islands, this species bears long, thin, branched floral stems with few flowers, laxly arranged on the stem. The white or green flowers usually have a little color near the base of the lip under the column.

Polyradicion lindenii, the ghost orchid from the Florida Everglades, the Bahamas, and Cuba

AERANGIDINAE

There are 36 tropical African genera in this subtribe of the Vandeae. The flower size and color vary, but the majority are white and usually have spurs. There are some aphyllous (leafless) species in this subtribe (for example, *Microcoelia gilpinae* to the right), in which the roots function like leaves.

Aerangis curnowiana
The long spur of this native of Madagascar forms as a circle in the bud, unfurling as it opens. The flower, sometimes occurring in a pure white form, is typical of *Aerangis*.

Podangis dactyloceras
The green anther caps can be seen through the glistening white, almost transparent floral segments. Even the spur is almost transparent.

Chamaeangis hariotiana
'WILLOW POND', CCM/AOS
This native of the Comoros Islands in the Indian Ocean produces large numbers of attractive flowers.

Pollinators of long-spurred flowers need a very long proboscis to reach the nectar at the base (not shown) of the spur

Tridactyle bicaudata
The three-(*tri*) lobed lip (*dactyle* means finger or lip) with two side lobes having two (*bi*) tails (*caudata*) is very unusual for this subtribe. From tropical Africa.

Rangaeris amaniensis
'LAURAY', CCM/AOS
Rangaeris is almost an anagram for *Aerangis* (see right); the name was selected probably because of the similarity between the genera.

Aerangis modesta
This native of Madagascar and the Comoros Islands has an unusual flowering habit: often the apical (end) flower opens first, making it the biggest on the stem.

Aerangis luteoalba var. *rhodosticta*
'HILDE', AM/AOS
Rhodosticta refers to the red dots (the columns) of these flowers. Up to 25 flowers may be borne, all neatly arranged in one plane.

Microcoelia gilpinae

PART
TWO

Eventually, many gardeners succumb to the allure of orchids and decide to grow a few (or a few thousand) in their gardens or greenhouses.

While many of them are not difficult to grow, like any other plant, orchids have specific cultural requirements that must be met to ensure good growth and bloom. For many gardeners, growing orchids leads to an interest in their preservation in the wild, to displaying them in shows, and to collecting the objects that celebrate their magical beauty.

Dendrochilum linearifolium
growing in its native habitat in the
Genting Highlands of Malaysia.

CONSERVATION

Orchids, along with many other plant and animal species, are disappearing forever at an alarming rate. Loss of habitat and over-collection from the wild are two principal factors in this trend. However, many organizations, among them the American Orchid Society and the Smithsonian Institution, along with other groups, such as the Nature Conservancy, the World Wildlife Fund, and the Center for Plant Conservation, as well as local orchid societies the world over, are working to save orchids and their native habitats.

TO BE OR NOT TO BE

Saving the plants
If the habitat cannot be saved, in some cases, the species growing there can be removed and replanted in private gardens, public preserves, or botanic gardens.

The end of their world
As rainforests and other natural habitats are destroyed, both the species themselves and their means to exist are lost. No one knows for sure how many species are now extinct.

Saving the habitat
Two powerful ways to ensure the continued existence of orchids in the wild is to help preserve their natural habitats and to refuse to purchase wild-collected plants.

WHAT YOU CAN DO

Anyone can play an important role in the conservation of orchids by:

1. Identifying orchid species that need protection in their area and alerting local authorities to them.

2. Becoming aware of CITES (Convention on International Trade in Endangered Species) and its role.

3. Purchasing only plants that have been certifiably propagated in nurseries.

4. Promoting the cultivation of seed-grown species to assure there will always be a diverse gene pool.

5. Supporting funding for research in methods of artificial propagation of endangered species.

6. Fostering the establishment and continuance, through funding or in-kind aid, of collections of orchid species in both private and research collections.

7. Educating growers by providing proper cultural information, including propagation.

8. Petitioning local and national governments to set aside more land for natural preserves.

9. Participating in the salvage and rescue of orchid species when practical or possible.

10. Helping your local orchid society to form a proactive conservation committee.

If all orchidophiles (from novice to expert growers) do their part and encourage others to follow suit, there will be native orchids in their natural habitats for generations to come.

Gigantic specimens of *Prosthechea baculas* in their native habitat near Volcan San Martin, Mexico

MEDIA AND POTTING

There are still many people who shy away from growing orchids, believing there is a mystique to success with these facinating plants. This is a shame, because orchids are no harder to grow than African violets. As long as they are grown under the right amount of light, provided the correct temperature, and properly watered and inspected, orchids will thrive and flower for years. The cultural practices given here, if followed, should enable anyone to grow a wide range of orchids.

——— TERRESTRIAL MEDIA ———

Like epiphytic orchids, terrestrial orchids (those that grow in soil in the wild) can be potted in a variety of media. A typical medium must contain organic matter (at least 40 percent by volume); hold water, yet be well drained; contain some nutrients; and, most important of all, be able to support the plant. Any medium that fulfills the above conditions can be used to grow terrestrial orchids. Terrestrial genera include *Calanthe*, *Cymbidium*, *Cypripedium*, *Paphiopedilum*, *Phaius*, and *Pleione*.

EPIPHYTIC MEDIA

Epiphytic orchids (those that grow on other plants in the wild) can be grown in a wide variety of media. Various combinations of barks (mainly fir), tree-fern fiber, perlite, sphagnum moss, peat moss, and cork bark are among the multitude of potting media used today. Epiphytic orchids can also be grown in hanging baskets or mounted on tree limbs or plaques made of cork or tree fern (see below). It has often been stated that epiphytic orchids can be grown in any medium except soil, as long as the grower's watering and fertilizing practices are adjusted for the medium. Epiphytic genera include *Cattleya*, *Dendrobium*, *Epidendrum*, *Miltonia*, *Oncidium*, *Phalaenopsis*, *Pleurothallis*, and *Vanda*.

Ground bark can be used alone or in mixes

Tree fern is long lasting and well aerated

Peatmoss combines easily with other media

Perlite is lightweight; promotes good aeration and drainage

50/50 mix of peat and perlite is good for most orchids

MOUNTING ORCHIDS

Cork slabs and tree fern cut into various shapes simulate the plants and surfaces that many orchids grow on naturally.

Epiphytic orchids thrive on cork bark, which lasts for years

Tree-fern plaque for mounting orchids

Tree-fern "pot"

Totem pole for tall or multiple plants

Many of the smaller species and hybrids grow superbly when mounted, and they can be easily moved around.

WHEN TO REPOT AN ORCHID

The growth type partially dictates how and when to repot a particular kind of orchid.

MONOPODIAL ORCHIDS

Since monopodial growth is vertical by nature, repotting is necessary only when the medium decomposes or when the plant becomes too tall for the container to support it. Otherwise, monopodials can be repotted any time they are in active growth. Some can be grown without any medium in a hanging basket. Examples of monopodials: *Phalaenopsis* and *Vanda*.

SYMPODIAL ORCHIDS

The horizontal growth of this type soon outgrows its container. It usually takes two years before a plant grows out of its pot; repot into a larger container that will allow for two more years' growth. The best time to repot this group is immediately after flowering or when new roots are just emerging from the base of the new growth (see right). Examples: *Cattleya, Oncidium.*

TELLTALE SIGNS

This sympodial orchid is giving two indications that the time is right to repot:
1. New shoot and root growth has extended beyond the pot rim.
2. Green-tipped new roots are beginning to elongate. Note: because roots are brittle and break easily, it is best to repot before the new roots are more than 1.5in (4cm) long.

REPOTTING AN ORCHID

1 This plant has produced a congested mass of roots and a large amount of top growth. Remove rotten or dead, dry roots, then divide into pieces.

2 The new divisions should consist of a few younger, healthy shoots. Cut away older and dead shoots with a sharp, sterilized knife or shears.

3 Make certain the new pot is large enough to allow for at least two years' growth. Choose a medium suitable for the nature of the orchid (see left).

4 Place the division in the pot with the oldest growth against the side of the pot, then fill with medium. Many growers use a stick to firm it.

CONTAINERS

Orchids can be grown in a wide variety of containers, some of which are shown here. Experienced growers use as few types as is practical, because the more types of container and materials used, the more complicated watering becomes. The ideal growing setup uses one type of pot and one type of hanging unit.

Hanging baskets should last for several years and are ideal for growing vandaceous orchids and pendent types

Clay pots allow moisture to evaporate from the medium, promoting root growth

Plastic pots are lightweight and require less frequent watering than clay, but they become brittle over time

PROPAGATION

Orchids, just like many other plants, can be propagated sexually (by seed) or asexually (using plant parts other than seeds). Growing orchids from seed is a complicated and time-consuming process. Asexual methods of propagating orchids are more often employed by the small grower. Division of sympodial orchids (see the repotting sequence on p. 143) and tip cuttings of monopodial orchids are the most commonly used techniques.

KEIKIS

A number of orchid genera (for example, *Dendrobium* and *Phalaenopsis*) produce vegetative offsets, called keikis, from the Hawaiian word for "little child." They arise from the stems or from an inflorescence. Once they have produced several roots more than 1in (2.5cm) long they can be removed from the parent and potted up.

Keiki arising from an inflorescence

Keiki is ready to be potted up

GROWING FROM SEED

Raising orchids from seed is not a technique the average hobby grower will find convenient or even possible. The minute seeds must be germinated under sterile conditions, and many require three to five years or more to become bloomimg-size plants. Some growers and hybridizers send their seeds to laboratories, which then return plantlets.

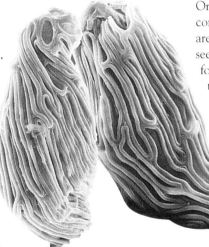

Orchid seeds are minute and contain no stored food. They are so small it would take 300 seeds, standing end to end, to form a line 1in (2.5cm) long. In the wild they rely on a specific kind of fungus to germinate, so they are produced in vast quantities to increase the chances of a few growing and reproducing.

However, seeds can be readily germinated in a laboratory using nutrient agar, first developed in 1922.

This ripe capsule (seed pod) has split open. It contains as many as one million seeds like the two pictured at left.

1 Upon receiving a flask of seedlings, assemble the materials needed: container, medium, hammer, and paper.

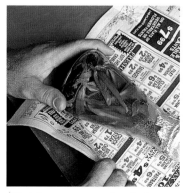

2 After wrapping the flask in the paper and carefully breaking the flask, remove the mass of plants from the glass.

3 Rinse the plants with tepid water to dissolve the jellylike agar and remove any glass shards that may remain.

4 Transfer the seedlings into what is called a community pot. Transplant separately when the plants outgrow the pot.

BASIC CARE

In addition to repotting (p. 143), orchids require the same growth factors as other plants. Given here are some very basic guidelines; for further information consult local orchid growers or the American Orchid Society (p. 160).

LIGHT

Both the kind (quality) and the amount (quantity) of light are important factors. Individuals growing orchids outdoors or in suitably covered greenhouses do not need to be concerned about light quality, because the sun's rays contain all the necessary light waves to ensure good growth. However, if orchids are grown indoors, for example under fluorescent lights in the basement, quality becomes a major consideration and can make the difference between success and failure.

Quantity of light depends on many variables, including geographical location, orientation toward the sun, time of day, the season, and the material under which plants are grown (if any), for instance glass, plastic, lath, or fluorescent lights. Fortunately, most orchids will grow well over a range of light intensities. In general, most genera will grow well at light levels between 2,400 and 3,000 foot-candles.

TEMPERATURE

Since orchids are native to all continents, as a family they grow naturally under a wide range of temperatures. However, observation and research over the years has led to the creation of three basic temperature groups. The chart below indicates the night temperature at which many of the most popular genera grow best. As with their light requirements, most orchids will grow well over a wide range of temperatures. The chart below gives recommended night temperatures.

HIGH 65 °F (18 °C)	INTERMEDIATE 60 °F (16 °C)	COOL 50 - 55 °F (10 - 13 °C)
•Aerangis •Aerides •Angraecum •Arachnis •Ascocentrum •Cymbidiella •Phalaenopsis •Rhynchostylis •Vanda •Vandopsis	•Bulbophyllum •Cattleya •Dendrobium •Laelia •Masdevallia •Miltonia •Oncidium •Paphiopedilum •Phalaenopsis •Vanda	•Angraecum •Anguloa •Bulbophyllum •Dracula •Dendrobium •Masdevallia •Oncidium •Odontoglossum •Paphiopedilum •Pleurothallis

WATERING

Proper watering is by far the most important aspect of orchid culture. It has been stated that more orchids are killed by improper watering than by any other factor.

It is impossible to provide a rule of thumb for how often to water a specific orchid. Temperature, light, and relative humidity vary from one location to another, within a given location, and from one part of the year (and even day) to the next. Generally, the higher the temperature and light, the more water is required, and the lower the humidity, the more frequently watering needs to be done.

A few plants can be easily watered at a sink.

A watering wand is very useful for watering a large collection.

The best rule is to water thoroughly; that is, to pour water onto all of the medium in the pot until the water runs out the bottom. This not only assures that all the medium in the pot is moistened but also leaches out some of the excess fertilizer salts, thus preventing damage from their buildup. Having thoroughly watered, do not water again until the top .5in (1.2cm) of medium is dry to the touch.

FERTILIZERS AND FERTILIZATION

Fertilization is the most controversial and least researched aspect of orchid culture. A plethora of orchid fertilizers is available, so the question of "Which one should I use?" inevitably arises. The potting medium used determines the NPK (Nitrogen/Phosphorus/Potassium) ratio, with bark requiring higher amounts of nitrogen (a 3-1-1 ratio) than peat and perlite, where a 1-1-1 ratio is needed. Applying one of these once a month, at the levels recommended on the container, will produce fine orchids plants and flowers. However, any balanced orchid fertilizer should produce very good plants.

It is most important to follow the directions on the fertilizer container, because the adage "If a teaspoonful is good, then two teaspoonfuls are better" does not hold in fertilizing orchids.

PESTS AND DISEASES

Sooner or later, every orchid grower will encounter an insect or disease problem. Usually, the problems are minor and easy to control. The best preventive measure is to inspect your plants, daily if possible, looking for problems and dealing with them before they become serious. For example, if you find scale on the underside of a leaf, remove it before it spreads to the next leaf or plant.

BOISDUVAL SCALE
This is the most common scale insect found on orchids. Unlike mealybugs (below), scale are hard-shelled and are mobile only when young. A severe scale infestation such as this can kill the plant.

Ants carry aphids around the plant and often establish them on other plants

When the ants move on, they leave most of the aphids behind

APHIDS (PLANT LICE)
Aphids usually attack young, succulent growth and flower buds and can cause considerable damage as they suck out the plant sap. Their numbers can increase rapidly in warm, dry weather. They are often "pastured" by ants for their secretion called honeydew, which the ants collect as food.

SLUGS
Slugs and snails (essentially slugs with a shell) can severely damage orchid buds and flowers. Although these pests often go undetected because they feed at night, shiny slime trails on the plants betray their presence.

MEALYBUGS
These mobile, soft-bodied scalelike insects (see above) often build up unnoticed because they hide in the growing points where new leaves and flower buds emerge, in leaf axils, and even among the roots.

CONTROLLING PESTS AND DISEASES
An ounce of prevention is often worth a pound of cure. However, if a given pest or disease becomes serious or does not respond to hand removal, there are other methods, including the use of chemicals, that will control the problem. Local orchid growers and the American Orchid Society are helpful resources for this and other aspects of orchid culture. In some cases, particularly when a plant is infected with a virus, the best treatment is to discard the plant to protect your other plants.

COLOR BREAK VIRUS
Irregularly colored ("broken") floral segments on this *Cattleya* indicate this virus disease. Symptoms are present only when the plant is in flower.

VIRUS
A number of viruses attack orchids (also see left), some of which produce leaf symptoms. Some viruses show no symptoms or look like fungal infestations.

DRY SEPAL
Ethylene gas, often produced during incomplete burning of heating fuel, causes sepal damage. Other airborne gases can also be damaging.

Caterpillars can quickly spoil the beauty of an orchid flower.

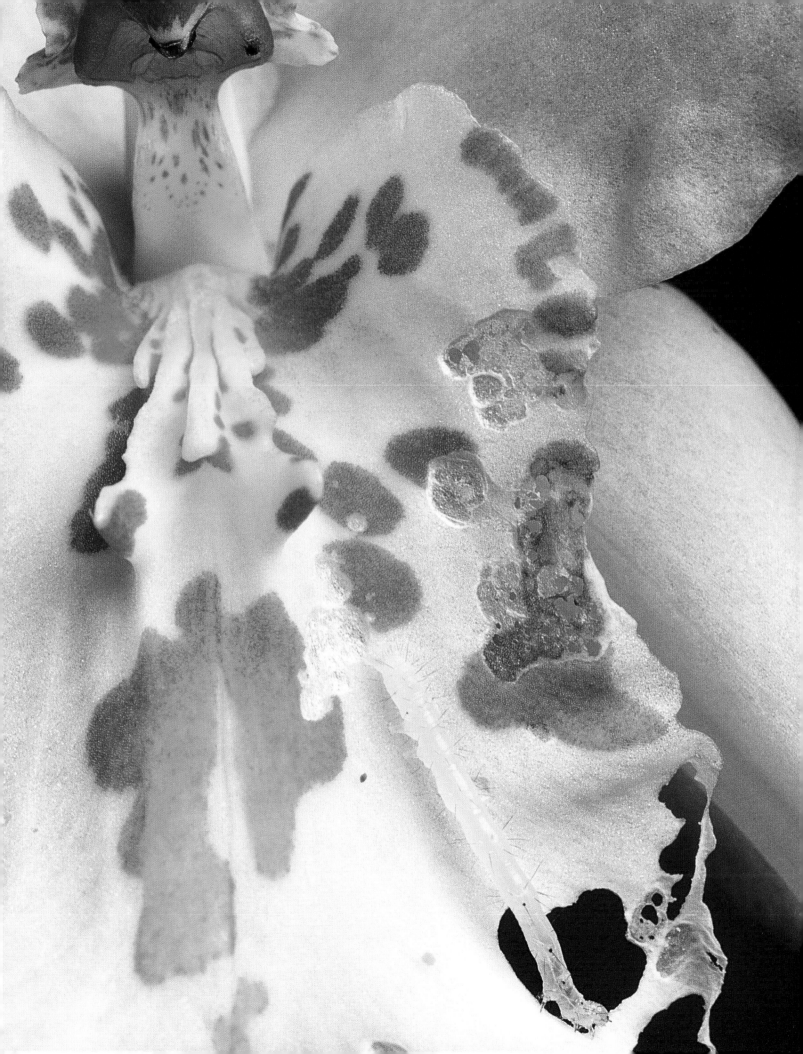

WHERE TO GROW ORCHIDS

Almost anyone has a spot that can be used for growing orchids, whether in a greenhouse, your home, or in favorable locations outdoors. As long as you provide the necessary environmental conditions, orchids will thrive.

GREENHOUSES AND SIMILAR STRUCTURES

Greenhouses come in a wide array of designs, sizes, and materials. They can be lean-tos, attached to the home, or free-standing and covered with glass, fiberglass, or plastic (either rigid or film). Size and type of covering depend specific cultural needs and, of course, budget. A free-standing 10 x 16ft (3.3 x 5.3m) greenhouse is ideal for a beginner.

OUTDOORS
If you live in a subtropical or tropical climate, orchids will thrive outdoors, provided their specific cultural needs are met.

Most hobbyists' home greenhouses are relatively small and usually contain a wide variety of species and hybrids. It is rare to find one devoted to a single genus.

A large commercial greenhouse can produce thousands of salable cut flowers and plants per year and requires large amounts of capital and effort. These *Phalaenopsis* are typical of what you could see if you visited a commercial greenhouse during peak bloom season.

Unheated shade houses or lath houses are ideal in tropical and subtropical areas. In temperate areas, they must be enclosed and heated in winter.

SUPPLEMENTAL LIGHTING

In some instances, especially when growing in the home, plants may not receive sufficient sunlight for good growth because of the absence of suitable windows (such as the one shown below) or an area's distance from windows. Providing supplemental light can solve the problem. A variety of lamps are on the market, or you can combine incandescent and fluorescent lighting to suit your needs and those of your plants.

Overhead fluorescent lighting supplements the natural light coming through the windows. Note how close some of the plants are to the lights.

The grower of this collection adapted his attic to accommodate his hobby. Natural light and additional lighting provide the correct conditons.

GROWING ON A WINDOWSILL

For many hobby growers, a windowsill offers sufficient space to grow their entire collection of plants. Any window can be used as long as direct rays of strong sun do not reach the plants. A sheer curtain can be placed between the plants and the window to filter the sun's rays.

ORCHID SHOWS AND AWARDS

Many orchid growers extend their hobby by exhibiting their plants in orchid shows. Sponsored by local, national, and international orchid societies around the world, they offer growers the opportunity to display their efforts to their peers and the public and to receive recognition in the form of ribbons and trophies. The American Orchid Society (AOS) encourages its Affiliated Societies (more than 550 worldwide) to stage shows by providing each society with a trophy for the most outstanding exhibit, as well as certified judges to evaluate everything in the show. The AOS also conducts an awards program that recognizes superior flowers and plants.

————SHOWS————

SEETING UP A DISPLAY
These gentlemen are determining where to place a plant to show it to best advantage and to make sure it does not break up the overall color and design flow of the exhibit or conceal other plants or flowers.

PRETTY AND INFORMATIVE
An orchid show is an attractive educational tool for both AOS members and the general public. Exhibitors are encouraged to label plants correctly with easily read name tags. Ribbons indicate the best flowers in a class.

————AWARDS————

THE JUDGE'S EYE
Judges accredited by the American Orchid Society evaluate orchid flowers and growers for a variety of awards (see below). Sessions are held throughout the year and across the country in 27 judging centers.

————AMERICAN ORCHID SOCIETY AWARDS————

The initials such as AM/AOS and JC/AOS following orchid names indicate awards bestowed by the judges of the American Orchid Society to worthy flowers, plants, and growers. See below for an explanation of the awards that occur as part of the name of many orchids in this book.

AD Award of Distinction and
AQ Award of Quality
These two awards for hybridizing in orchids recognize worthy new trends and improved quality, respectively.

AM Award of Merit
Given to a flower scoring 80 to 89 points on a scale of 100 points.

CBR Certificate of Botanical Recognition
Awarded to rare and unusual species with educational interest.

CCM Certificate of Cultural Merit
This award, rather than designating an individual flower of high quality, recognizes the grower and not the plant. The CCM

may be given more than once if the plant continues to thrive and increase in both the size and number of flowers.

CCE Certificate of Cultural Excellence
This award further distinguishes growers of plants that exhibit an extreme degree of skill in cultivation, having received 90 points or more on the CCM scale (above).

CHM Certificate of Horticultural Merit
Awarded to a well-grown and well-flowered species or natural hybrid with characteristics that contribute to the horticultural aspects of orchidology.

FCC First Class Certificate
The highest flower-quality award, given to

flowers scoring 90 or more points on a scale of 100 points. Only a very few orchids win this award each year.

HCC Highly Commended Certificate
The HCC is granted to a flower scoring 75 to 79 points on a scale of 100 points. The majority of awarded orchids receive this award, which implies that, while the flower being judged is outstanding, there is room for improvement.

JC Judges Commendation
Given to orchids that show distinctive characteristics that the AOS judges, by an affirmative vote of at least 75 percent, feel should be recognized but cannot be scored in customary ways.

Champion display by Mukoyama Orchids at the 2001 Tokyo Dome Grand Prix Show

COLLECTIBLES

Orchid memorabilia, or collectibles, are almost as popular as (and for some people more intriguing than) orchids themselves. Whether it be a product advertisement adorned with a *Cattleya*, a piece of sterling silver flatware embossed with a *Phalaenopsis*, a china plate featuring a native *Cypripedium*, or any of a multitude of other items, there are collectors looking for it to add to their troves. One arguable benefit: unlike orchid plants, orchid collectibles never need water or fertilizer, and they are in flower all the time.

MONEY

Currency, like stamps, is issued and collected around the world. This paper money from Singapore features vandaceous orchids in full color. Each denomination in the series pictures a different orchid.

JEWELRY

For centuries, orchids have inspired jewelry designers to create exquisite pieces in silver, gold, cloisonne, and many other materials. The enameled and jewel-studded orchids to the right, made by Tiffany & Co., were part of a larger exhibit at the Paris Exposition Universelle in 1889.

Three large stones represent the anther cap

The column is adorned with precious stones, as is the peduncle (floral stem)

The artwork was inspired by a Cattleya

These stamps depict orchid hybrids from the Eric Young Orchid Foundation on the Isle of Jersey, England

STAMPS

Many countries have issued a multitude of stamps depicting orchids. Some enthusiasts create topical collections devoted strictly to orchids.

CHINA AND GLASS

Royal Copenhagen, Limoges, Lenox, and many other companies have long featured orchids on their wares. Paden City Glass Co., Paden City, West Virginia produced a line of clear glassware in seven different colors etched with orchid flowers. These pieces are highly collectible today. The cake plate above is from the line called Paden City Orchid 2.

A gold- and silver-inlaid bowl depicting Polyradicion lindenii, *the ghost orchid, by Marion Ruff Sheehan*

GLOSSARY

A

alliance A group of similar genera, for example the *Cattleya* Alliance.

anther cap The covering of the pollen massses on the flower's column.

aphyllous Without leaves.

apical At or pertaining to the tip of any structure.

aseptic Free from disease organisms.

asexual Without involving sex, such as in vegetative propagation.

attenuated Narrowing to a point.

axil The angle between a branch or a leaf and the stem or axis from which it arises.

B

backbulb An old pseudobulb, frequently used for propagation, behind the actively growing portion.

bifoliate Having two leaves.

bigeneric Involving two distinct genera in the parentage of a hybrid.

blade The expanded portion of a leaf or floral segment.

botanical A term designating any species or genus of orchid not grown commercially for its flowers.

bract A reduced leaflike or scalelike organ embracing the base of a stem, flower, or group of flowers.

C

callus A hard protuberance or thickening, usually on orchid lips (plural: calli).

capsule A dry dehiscent fruit composed of more than one carpel; the seed pod.

cauda A slender tail-like appendage (plural: caudae).

caudicle A slender stalklike appendage of the pollinium or pollen mass.

clone An individual plant raised from a single seed, plus all of its subsequent vegetative propagations.

cluster A group of flowers or leaves in close proximity to one another.

column The central organ of the orchid flower, formed by the union of the stamens and pistils.

crest A toothed, fringed, or hairy thickened portion of the lip.

crispate Finely wavy along the edge.

cross To transfer pollen from a flower to the flower of a different plant; the progeny resulting from such pollination.

cultivar An individual plant and its vegetative propagations in cultivation; a horticultural variety.

D

dormant In a period of inactivity; not in active growth.

dorsal sepal The upper sepal (outer floral segment) on orchid flowers.

E

endemic Native to a particular region, as a country or an island, and not found elsewhere.

epiphyte A plant that naturally grows on another plant above the soil but deriving its needed moisture from the air.

F

family The usual major subdivision of an order or suborder, commonly consisting of a group of related genera, ending with –aceae, as in Orchidaceae.

fringed Furnished with hairlike appendages on the edges.

foot-candle A unit of illumination equivalent to that produced by a standard candle at the distance of one foot.

G

generic Of or pertaining to a genus, as in a generic name such as *Cattleya*.

genus A subdivision of a family, consisting of one or more species that show similar characteristics and have an assumed common ancestry (plural: genera).

grex A flock or group, applied collectively to the offspring of a given cross.

H

hirsute Covered with long, rather coarse or stiff hairs.

hybrid The offspring resulting from the union of a species or hybrid with another species or hybrid.

I

inflorescence The general arrangement and disposition of the flowers on an axis; the flowering part of a plant.

intergeneric Between or among two or more genera.

introduced Brought from another region, either intentionally or otherwise.

K

keel A central dorsal ridge, like the keel of a boat, usually on the lip of orchids.

keiki Hawaiian term used by orchidists to signify an adventitious offshoot from an orchid's cane (stem) or inflorescence.

L

labellum The lip or modified petal of an orchid flower.

lateral sepals The two lower sepals.

lip see labellum

lithophyte A plant that grows on rocks.

lobe Any division or segment of an organ, such as a leaf or petal.

M

medium (1) A nutrient substance on which orchid seeds are germinated. (2) The substance or substratum in which an orchid plant is grown.

monopodial A form of growth in which there is a single vegetative shoot that continues in growth from its terminal bud from season to season, such as in the genus *Vanda*.

multigeneric Composed of many genera; usually used in reference to hybrids combining several genera in a hybrid.

mycorrhizal Having symbiotic fungi associated with roots, the usual condition in orchids.

N

node A joint on a stem or pseudobulb that normally bears a bract, a leaf, a whorl of leaves, or a root.

nomenclature A set or system of names and naming.

nonresupinate Said of flowers with the lip uppermost.

O

ovary The part of an orchid flower that becomes the fruit following pollination and fertilization.

ovate Shaped like the outline of an egg, with the broader end downward.

P

panicle A loosely arranged branched inflorescence, blooming from the center or lower branches to the outer ends or top.

pedicel The stalk of an individual flower. In orchids, the pedicel is usually continuous with the inferior ovary.

peduncle The stalk of an inflorescence that bears the pedicels and flowers.

peloric Having petals similar to the lip or a lip similar to the petals.

pendent Hanging or drooping.

perennial Having a life cycle lasting more than two years.

petal One of the segments of the corolla of a flower; in orchids, one of the three petals is usually modified into a labellum (lip).

petiole The stalk by which a leaf is attached to a stem.

phylad A branch or limb of a family tree.

plicate Folded like a fan, or pleated.

pollinium A mass of waxy pollen found in the anthers of most orchids (plural: pollinia).

pollinarium The inclusive term for the pollination unit of most orchids.

polyploid Having more than two chromosome sets in each somatic cell.

pouch The bootlike lip on some orchids.

primary hybrid A cross made between two species.

pseudobulb A thickened portion of a stem, resembling a bulb but not being a true bulb.

pseudocopulation A false mating, for example between an insect and a flower.

R

raceme A simple inflorescence of stalked flowers on a common, more or less elongated axis.

resupinate With the lip on the lower side of the flower in respect to the rachis.

rhizome A root-bearing stem, prostrate or under the ground, the apex (tip) of which progressively sends up leafy shoots.

rostellum A sometimes beaklike extension of the stigma that produces a viscous substance used in pollination.

S

segment A part of the perianth, as the petal, sepal, or lip; any division or part of a cleft or divided organ.

sepal One of the divisions of the calyx; one of the three outer parts of an orchid flower.

sepaline Belonging to or consisting of the sepals.

sessile Attached directly by the base, without a stalk.

sheath A protective leaflike growth that envelops the stem, especially the flattened covering that protects the developing inflorescence in genera such as *Cattleya*.

species (singluar and plural) A group of organisms showing integradation among its individuals and having in common one or more characteristics that definitely separate it from any other group.

spike A type of inflorescence with sessile (stalkless) flowers, or short-stalked flowers borne on an upright, unbranched flower stem.

spray A term for an inflorescence.

spur A hollow, saclike or tubular extension of the base of the lip, often bearing nectar.

stigma The part of the pistil of a flower that is receptive to pollen.

stigmatic Pertaining to the stigma.

stipe The stalklike support of a pollinium.

subfamily A group of genera (within a family) believed to have a common origin.

subtribe Taxonomic category below a tribe, ending in –inae.

sympodial A form of growth in which each new shoot, originating from a bud of the rhizome, is complete in itself and terminates in a potential inflorescence, such as in the genus *Cattleya*.

synsepal The ventral portion of the flower of the slipper orchids (*Paphiopedilum*) formed by the fusion of the lateral sepals.

T

terete Cylindrical; circular in cross-section (as in terete-leaved).

terrestrial Growing in the ground and supported by soil.

tessellated Arranged in a checkered or mosaic pattern.

tribe A primary taxonomic category of related genera, or the fundamental division of an order.

trigeneric Of or pertaining to three genera, usually applied in reference to hybrids derived from the combination of three parent genera.

tubercle A small tuber or tuberlike body, not necessarily subterranean.

U

undulate With a wavy edge or surface.

unifoliate One-leaved.

V

variegated Irregularly colored in patches; blotched.

variety A subset (of a population) having minor characteristics that distinguish it from the typical members of the species.

velamen The layer (or layers) of cells covering the roots of epiphytic orchids that aids in the rapid absorption and assimilation of water and mineral nutrients.

viscidium The sticky base of the stipe or caudicle that affixes the pollinarium to a pollinator (such as an insect).

Z

zygomorphic Capable of being divided into symmetrical halves in one plane only as in the flowers of orchids; bilaterally symmetrical.

INDEX

A

Acineta hennisiana 'Socrates', CHM/AOS, **122**
Aerangidinae, **136–137**
Aerangis, 145
    curnowiana, **5, 136**
    luteoalba var. *rhodosticta* 'Hilde', AM/AOS, **136**
    modesta, **136**
Aeranthes
    grandiflora 'Schnurmacher', HCC/AOS, **134**
    ramosa, **134**
Aerides, 96, 145
    crassifolia, **132**
    flabellatum, **92**
Aeridinae, **132–133**
Aeridovanda
    Arnold Sanchez 'Butterball', HCC/AOS, **97**
    Barney Garrison 'Aileen', AM/AOS, **97**
    Fuchs Jewell 'Robert', AM/AOS, **97**
American Orchid Society (AOS), 7, 148, 160
    awards, 38, 84, 94, 150
    conservation, 140
    first meeting minutes, **7**
    nomenclature protocol, 13
    orchid registration, 106
Angraecinae, **134–135**
Angraecum, 145
    eichlerianum, **134**
    leonis, **16–17**
    sesquipedale 'Estrella Blanca', HCC/AOS, **134**
Anguloa, 120, 145
    cliftonii, **120**
    clowesii, **120**
    x*rolfei*, **110**
    tognettiae, **120**
Angulocaste Rosemary, **120**
Ansellia africana var. *natalensis*, **116**
ants, **146**
aphids (plant lice), **146**
Arachnis, 96
Arethusa bulbosa, **124**
Arethusinae, **124**
Armacost and Royston, 9
Arpophyllinae, **126**
Arpophyllum giganteum 'Santa Barbara', CCE/AOS, **126**
art, orchids in, 35, **152–153**
Ascocenda
    Crownfox Golden Dawn 'Miramar', AM/AOS, **95**
    Meda Arnold, 94
    Motes Hot Chestnut 'Tony Betancourt', HCC/AOS, **86**
    Natalie Majewski 'Norma', AM/AOS, **94**
    Paki Long 'Redland Sunspots', HCC/AOS, **94**
    Portia Doolittle, 94
    Suksamran Spots 'Suni', AM/AOS, **94**
    Thai Friendship 'Mary Motes', AM/AOS, **94**
    Yip Sum Wah 'Tomato', AM/AOS, **94**
Ascocentrum, 96, 145
    ampullaceum 'Aida Cruz', CCM/AOS, **93**
    miniatum (orange variant), **92**
    miniatum (yellow variant), **92**
award categories, 150

B

Barbosella australis (*cucullata*), **74**
basic care, 145
Bifrenaria tyranthina, **120**
Bletia purpurea (*verecunda*), 8
Bletiinae, **124**
Blume, Karl, 100
Boisduval scale, **146**
Boott, John and James, 9

Botanicals, **110–137**
Brass, William, 48
Brassavola, 60, 66
    cucullata, **11**
    nodosa, **60**
Brassia, 48
    Chieftain 'Big Lou', JC/AOS, **49**
    Spider's Gold 'Hilo Orchid Farm', AM/AOS, **48**
Brassocattleya
    Binosa 'Wabash Valley', AM/AOS, **6, 60**
    Mount Adams, 60
Brassolaeliocattleya
    Chyong Guu Chaffinch 'Dixie's Joy', HCC/AOS, **61**
    Goldfield 'Bronze Prince', **60**
    Lester McDonald 'Meadow', HCC/AOS, **60**
    Norman's Bay 'Gothic', AM/AOS, **60**
Broughtonia sanguinea, 66
Brown, Robert, 48, 112
Bulbophyllinae, **128–131**
Bulbophyllum, 132, 145
    aemulum 'Wappingers Falls', CHM/AOS, **130**
    annandalei 'D & B', CHM/AOS, **128**
    auratum 'Other World', CHM/AOS, **130**
    barbigerum, **128**
    binnendijkii 'Odoriferously Magnifico', CHM/AOS, **128**
    falcatum var. *bufo*, **130**
    frostii, **130**
    lemniscatoides 'Wappingers Falls', CBR/AOS, **128**
    lishanensis, **128**
    Louis Sander, **128**
    makoyanum, 128, **131**
    medusae, **129**
    phalaenopsis, **128**
    robustum (*graveolens*) 'Castle', AM/AOS, **130**
    roseopunctatum 'Patricia', CHM/AOS, **130**
    rothschildianum 'A-Doribil', CCM/AOS, **128**
    wendlandianum, **130**
"bulldog" orchids, 19
"bullfrog" orchids, 19

C

Caladenia
    catenata, **112**
    dilatata, **112**
Calanthe
    vestita, **124**
    Victoria Katrina 'Red Eye', **124**
California, orchid commerce in, 9, 35
Calochilus robertsonii, **112**
Calopogon tuberosus, **124**
Catasetum
    barbatum, **116**
    fimbriatum, **116**
    schmidtianum 'Crown Fox', CHM/AOS, **116**
    tenebrosum 'Clown Alley', JC/AOS, **111, 116**
caterpillars, **147**
Cattley, William, 9, 54
Cattleya, 15, 44, 143, 145
    aclandiae, **56**
    aclandiae 'Joe Elmore', HCC/AOS, **55**
    anatomy, 11
    aurantiaca, 54, 56, 62
    aurantiaca 'Mario Palmieri Di Pollina', AM/AOS, **54**
    bicolor, 56, 60, 62
    bicolor 'Denise', JC/AOS, **55**
    Bow Bells, 56
    Brabantiae 'Trinity Bay', HCC/AOS, **56**
    Chocolate Drop, 54
    Chocolate Drop 'Bittersweet', HCC/AOS, **56**

    dowiana, 54, 60
    dowiana 'Midas Touch', AM/AOS, **55**
    guttata, 54, 56
    Helene Garcia, 54, **56**
    Hybrida, 15, **56**
    intermedia var. *orlata* 'Crownfox Jewel', FCC/AOS, **55**
    Iris, **56**
    labiata, 9, 54, 56, 60
    labiata 'Goliath', AM/AOS, **54**
    loddigesii, **56**
    loddigesii 'Beaver Valley', AM/AOS, **55**
    luteola, **62**
    mossiae, 54, 60, 62
    mossiae var. *semi-alba* 'Canaima's Niki', HCC/AOS, **54**
    Panache Amphora 'Waltari Wine', HCC/AOS, **57**
    Pearl Harbor 'Orchidglade', AM/AOS, **56**
    Portiata 'Streeter's Choice', HCC/AOS, **56**
    trianaei, **54**
    trianaei 'Mooreana', AM/AOS, **54**
    walkeriana, **62**
Cattleya Alliance, 13, **52–67**
Center for Plant Conservation, 140
Chamaeangis hariotiana 'Willow Pond', CCM/AOS, **136**
characteristics of orchids, five main, **10–11**
Charlesworth and Company, 44
china and glass, **152–153**
Christieara
    Crownfox Magic Lantern, **87**
    Fuchs Confetti 'Robert', HCC/AOS, **97**
    Michael Tibbs 'Redland', FCC/AOS, **96**
    Renee Gerber 'Fuchs Spotty', AM/AOS, **97**
Cirrhopetalum, 128
classification, **12–13**
Cochleanthes
    Amazing 'Donnan', AM/AOS, **118**
    amazonica, **118**
    anatomy, 11
cocktail orchids, 62
Coelogyne
    cristata, **126**
    pandurata, **126**
Coelogyninae, **126**
collectibles, **152–153**
Collinson, Peter, 8
Colmanara Wildcat 'Alan J. Davidson', AM/AOS, **50**
color break virus, **146**
column (gynandrium), 10
commerce, 9, 35, 77, 82, 90
Confucius, 8
conservation, **140–141**
containers, **143**
Convention on International Trade in Endangered Species (CITES), 140
Corybas carinatus, **113**
cradle orchids, **120**
Cryptostylis conspicua, **112**
cultivars, 15
cultivation, 8–9, **142–149**
Cycnoches Pentawar 'Gail', AM/AOS, **117**
Cymbidieae, **116–117**
Cymbidiella pardalina, **116**
Cymbidioids, **116–123**
Cymbidium
    African Sky 'Savannah', HCC/AOS, **39**
    canaliculatum (Queensland type), **37**
    Castle Rock 'Orange Magic', **39**
    Church Creek 'Painted Lady', **39**
    Cracker Jack 'Santa Barbara', **38**
    devonianum, **38**
    Eburneo-lowianum, 38
    Eleanor Rigby 'Harmony', HCC/AOS, **38**

erythrostylum 'Magnificum', **36**
finlaysonianum, 35
hookerianum 'Loyola', HCC/AOS, **36**
John Wooden 'Bruin', AM/AOS, **34**
kanran 'Makino', **36**
lancifolium, **36**
lowianum, 38
lowianum 'Concolor', CBR/AOS, **36**
lowianum var. *lowianum* 'Comte D'Hemptinne',
    CHM/AOS, **4**, **36**
Mendocino 'Shamrock', **39**
Mescal Ridge 'California', **38**
Orchid Conference 'Green Cascade', **38**
Phar Lap 'Ruby Glow', AM/AOS, **38**
Rocky Point 'Brownie', **38**
sinense, **35**, **36**
Tarpy Flats 'Jazz Festival', **39**
Ventana Creek 'Highlights', **39**
cymbidiums, **34–39**
Cynorkis, 8
Cypripedium
    acaule, **32**
    californicum, **32**
    distribution, 19
    fasciculatum (green form), **32**
    formosanum 'Trident's Twinkle Toes',
        CCM/AOS, **32**
    macranthum, **32**
    parviflorum var. *pubescens*, **19**, **33**
    reginae, **32**

D

de Ferdinand, Baron Rothschild, 20
Dendrobium, **76–85**, 132, 145
    antennatum var. *d'albertisii*, **80**
    bullenianum (*topaziacum*), **79**, 84
    chrysotoxum 'Susanne', CCM/AOS, **78**
    crumenatum, 77
    Crystal Pink 'Rhon-Ron', HCC/AOS, **84**
    cucumerinum, **78**
    cuthbertsonii, 77
    cuthbertsonii 'Blaze', AM/AOS, **80**
    densiflorum, **78**
    distribution, 77
    Doctor Poyck 'Ryan's Grand Slam', AM/AOS, **84**
    Dominianum, 82
    gouldii, 84
    Haleahi Stripes 'Chi', JC/AOS, **84**
    harveyanum, 77
    Jesmond Treasure 'Spider', **84**
    johannis, 84
    King Dragon 'Montclair', HCC/AOS, **82**
    Kirsch 'Lady Hamilton', 84
    Kuranda Classic 'Quick', AM/AOS, **82**
    laevifolium 'Marcella', AM/AOS, **80**
    lawesii, 84
    linawianum, 82
    Malones 'Hope,' **82**
    Mount Fuji, **76**
    nobile, 78, **80**, 82
    Pale Doreen 'Guo Luen', HCC/AOS, **82**
    phalaenopsis, 78, 82, 84
    Roy Yahiro 'Orchid Acres Stephanie',
        HCC/AOS, **83**
    smillieae, **81**
    speciosum var. *hillii* 'El Queso Grande',
        CCM/AOS, **78**
    spectabile, 80
    Star of Gold, **80**, **85**
    Summer Sunrise, **84**
    superbum, 77
    tetragonum, **80**
    thyrsiflorum, **78**
    tixieri, 77
    tobaense 'Jolly Green Elf', HCC/AOS, **80**
    Touch of Gold 'T. J.', HCC/AOS, **84**

    unicum, **78**
    Yukidaruma 'King', AM/AOS, **82**
Dendrochilum
    linearifolium, **138–139**
    wenzelii, **126**
Diacattleya Chantilly Lace 'Buttons & Bows', **66**
Dioscorides, 8
Disa
    Noyo 'Blaze', **115**
    watsonii, **114**
diseases, **146**
Dominy, John, 56
Doritaenopsis
    Buena Lemon Brite 'Golden Glow',
        AM/AOS, **108**
    Kenneth Schubert 'Oriental Sky', HCC/AOS, **109**
    Malibu Bay 'Zuma Lipstick', AM/AOS, **108**
    Malibu Easter 'Iosco Butterfly', JC/AOS, **109**
    Maui Sizzle 'Mahalo Louie', HCC/AOS, **109**
    Mem. Val Rettig 'Wallbrunn', AM/AOS, **109**
    Nuevo Paraiso 'Squeaky', HCC/AOS, **109**
    Pinata 'Pacific', **109**
    Purple Gem 'Snow Court', HCC/AOS, **109**
    Red Pearl 'Barbara Ann', AM/AOS, **108**
    Sogo Maria 'Oriental Stripes', HCC/AOS, **99**
    Taisuco Candystripe 'Majestic Flare', JC/AOS, **109**
Doritis, 99, 108, 132
    pulcherrima 'A-Doribil', HCC/AOS, **108**
    pulcherrima 'Fred Jernigan', HCC/AOS, **108**
    pulcherrima 'June Snow', AM/AOS, **108**
dove orchid, 122, **123**
Dracula, 72, 145
    simia 'Racha', HCC/AOS, **73**
    sodiroi, 72
Dracuvallia Blue Boy No. 2, 72
Dressler, Dr. Robert L., 12, 111
dry sepal, **146**

E

Easter orchid, 54
Elleanthus
    sphaerocephala 'Eichenfels Goozle', CBR/AOS, **127**
    trilobatus, **126**
Embreea rodegisiana, **122**
Encyclia
    cochleata 'Dancing Lady', HCC/AOS, **64**
    cordigera, 64
    cordigera 'Maurice', HCC/AOS, **64**
    tampensis, 64, 66
    tampensis 'Peggy', HCC/AOS, **53**
England, orchid commerce in, 8–9, 35, 54
environments for growing orchids, 69, 145, **148–149**
Epidendroids, **124–127**
Epidendrum
    Atropine 'FANGtastic', HCC/AOS, **64**
    Hokulea 'Firestorm', AM/AOS, **64**
    Hokulea 'Palmer Orchids', CCM/AOS, **64**
    ilense 'Lil', HCC/AOS, **64**
    medusae (*Nanodes medusae*), **65**
    pseudepidendrum 'Yasna', AM/AOS, **64**
    Tropical Bees 'Feuerbach', AM/AOS, **64**
Epilaeliocattleya
    Carolyn Contorno, **66**
    Kenneth Roberts 'Boon', HCC/AOS, **66**
epiphytic media, **142**
Eric Young Orchid Foundation, 152
Esmeralda clarkei 'Bokay', CHM/AOS, **132**
Euanthe, see *Vanda*, 88, 90
Eulophia guineensis, **116**
exhibitions, **150–151**

F

fertilizers and fertilization, 145
Fitzwilliam, Earl, 46

flask culture, **9**, **144**
Florida butterfly orchid, **53**
flowers, zygomorphic, 10
food properties of orchids, 8, 114
foxtail orchid, **92**

G

ghost orchid, 134, 135, **153**
glassware, **152**
greenhouses, **148**
grex, 15
growing orchids, **142–149**
gynandrium (column), 10

H

Habenaria carnea 'Orchid Man', CCM/AOS, **114**
habitat protection, 140
hanging baskets, **143**
Hawaii, orchid commerce, 9, 77, 82, 90
Hirose, Y., 9
historical background, 8–9
Holy Ghost orchid, 122, **123**
Hooker, W. J., 64
Humboldt, Bonpland, and Knuth, 48
Huntington, Henry E., 35
Huntleya gustavii 'Hatillo Star', AM/AOS, **118**
hyacinth orchid, **126**
hybrids, 15

J

jewelry, **152**
Jones, Sir William, 88
Jumellea arachnanthe, **134**

K

Kagawara Christie Lowe 'Redland', HCC/AOS, **97**
keikis, **144**
Kew Gardens, 8
Knudson, Louis, 9

L

labellum (lip), **11**
lady slipper orchids, **32–33**
Laelia, 145
    anatomy, 11
    anceps var. *veitchiana*, **58**
    cinnabarina, **62**
    crispa, 58, 62
    flava, 62
    harpophylla 'Sonoma', HCC/AOS, **59**
    pumila 'KG's Hot Ticket', HCC/AOS, **58**
    purpurata 'Neptune', AM/AOS, **14**
    purpurata var. *carnea* 'Howe', HCC/AOS, **14**
    purpurata var. *coerulea* 'Craig Reavis',
        AM/AOS, **14**
    purpurata var. *sanguinea* 'Twin Peaks',
        HCC/AOS, **14**
    purpurata var. *schusteriana* 'Purple Velvet',
        HCC/AOS, **14**
    purpurata var. *werkhauseri* 'Kathleen',
        AM/AOS, **52**
    rubescens 'Heart's Desire', CCM/AOS, **58**
    rubescens var. *aurea* 'Crownfox', HCC/AOS, **58**
    tenebrosa 'Veronica', AM/AOS, **58**
Laelia/Laelius, 58
Laeliocattleya
    Burnt Orange 'Firefly', **62**
    Copper Mark 'Copper Summit', AM/AOS, **63**
    Dormaniana, 62
    Elizabeth Chang 'Nishida', HCC/AOS, **63**
    Elizabeth Fulton, **63**

Harvest Moon 'Red Chocolate', **62**
Mem. Robert Strait 'Blue Hawaii', JC/AOS, **62**
Nigrescent, **63**
Orange Sherbet 'Robbie', HCC/AOS, **62**
Pixie 'Canary', **63**
Trick or Treat 'Orange Beauty', HCC/AOS, **62**
leis, making, **9**
Lepanthes
calodictyon 'Eichenfels', CHM/AOS, **74**
felis, **74**
lindleyana, **74**
medusa 'Shandoah's Piper', CBR/AOS, **75**
zamorensis 'Free Spirit', CBR/AOS, **69**
Lepanthopsis floripectin, **74**
light and lighting, **145**, **149**
Lindley, Dr. John, **8**, **9**, **12**, 46, 54, 58
Linnaeus (Carl von Linne), 32, 64
Loddiges, Messrs., **9**
Londesbrough, Lady Denison, 88
Low, Sir Hugh, 36
Lycaste
aromatica, **121**
cruentum, 120
fragrans 'Manzanita', CHM/AOS, **121**
fulvescens, 120
fulvescens 'Apricot Jam', CBR/AOS, **121**
locusta, **121**
plana, **121**
powellii, **121**
Shoalhaven 'Firestorm', **121**
Sunray 'Gunner', HCC/AOS, **121**
Lycastinae, 120–121

M

Masdevall, José, 70
Masdevallia, 69, 145
anatomy, 11
Charisma 'Keeno', **70**
coccinea, 70
deformis 'Perfecto', HCC/AOS, **68**
Falcon Sunrise, 70
ignea, 70
Pixie Lavender, **71**
Pixie Leopard 'Williamsburg's Jef', AM/AOS, **70**
Tanager 'Trader's Point', HCC/AOS, **70**
triangularis 'Alpha', **70**
veitchiana 'Macro', AM/AOS, **4**
Massachusetts Horticultural Society, 9
Maxillaria fractiflexa 'Sonoma', CHM/AOS, **122**
Maxillariinae, 122
mealybugs, 146
media, 142
medicinal properties of orchids, 8, 35, 114
memorabilia, 152–153
Microcoelia gilpinae, **137**
Microsaccus brevifolius, **132**
Miltassia Jungle Cat 'African Queen', HCC/AOS, **50**
Milton, Viscount, 46
Miltonia, 145
Arthur Cobbledick 'Snowfire', **46**
Arthur Cobbledick 'Strawberries and Cream', **47**
Beall's Apache Tears 'M', **40**
Bleuana, 46
Goodale Moir 'Golden Wonder', HCC/AOS, **46**
Jean Carlson 'Rosemoon', **46**
Rainbow Falls 'Raspberry', **47**
Robert Ness 'Harvest Moon', AM/AOS, **47**
roezlii, 46
Rouge 'Akatsuka', CCM/AOS, **46**
spectabilis var. *moreliana* 'Harford's Ebony Star', FCC/AOS, **47**
spectabilis var. *moreliana* 'Linda Dayan', HCC/AOS, **47**
vexillaria, 46
Miltoniopsis, 46
moccasin flower, 32

Mokara
Michael Coronado 'Fuchs Spots', AM/AOS, **97**
Redland Sunset 'Robert', AM/AOS, **96**
money, orchids on, 152
Mormolyca gracilipes, **122**
morphology, 10–11
mounting orchids, **142**
Mukoyama Orchids display, **151**
mule-ear oncidiums, 42

N

Nature Conservancy, 140
nomenclature, 13, 15, 150

O

Odontioda
Avranches 'Sal', AM/AOS, **50**
Mount Bingham, **50**
Odontocidium
Big Mac, **50**
Odontoglossum, 48
bictoniense (*Lemboglossum bictoniense*), 48
cariniferum, 48
crispum 'Sunset Lace', AM/AOS, **48**
Laura Hett 'Salma', AM/AOS, **41**
Midnight Miracles 'Michael Palermo', AM/AOS, **48**
praestans 'San Damiano', HCC/AOS, **48**
Rawdon Jester 'Happiness', **48**
Troilus 'Snow Leopard', **48**
Odontorettia Ronald Ciesinski 'Laguna Niguel', AM/AOS, **50**
Oeonia volucris, **134**
Oncidiinae, 41
Oncidium, 145
aurisasinorum, **42**
baueri, **42**
bifolium, 9, **43**
Cloud Ears 'Tall, Dark & Handsome', HCC/AOS, **44**
Elfin Star 'Puanani', AM/AOS, **44**
flexuosum, 9
Galveston Bay 'Chase', AM/AOS, **45**
Golden Sunset 'Brilliant', **44**
hintonii, **42**
Illustre, **44**
leucochilum, 42, **44**
macranthum 'Patience', AM/AOS, **1**
maculatum, 44
Sharry Baby 'Sweet Fragrance', AM/AOS, **44**
sylvestre 'Mid Michigan', HCC/AOS, **42**
trilobum 'Nancy K', HCC/AOS, **42**
Oncidium Alliance, 40–51
Ophrys
apifera, **114**
bommuelleri, **114**
ciliata (*vernixia*), **114**
lutea, **114**
orchid(s)
in art, 35, 152–153
basic care, 145
capsule (seed pod), **144**
collectibles, **152–153**
in commerce, 9, 35, 77, 82, 90
conservation, 140
containers, **143**
cultivation, 8–9, **142–149**
on currency, 152
fertilizers and fertilization, 145
food properties, 8, 114
growing media, **142**
historical background, 8–9
how to mount, **142**
light and lighting, 145, **147**
medicinal properties, 8, 35, 114
nomenclature, 13, 15, 150
origin of name, 8

pests and diseases, **146–147**
pollination strategies, 112, 114, 116, 134, 136
propagation, **144**
repotting, **143**
shows and awards, 150–151
stamps, 152
temperature, 145
watering, **145**
where to grow, 148–149
Orchidaceae, classification, 12–13
Orchidoideae, **112–115**
Orchis mascula, **114**

P

Paden City Orchid 2, 152
Paphinia cristata, **122**
Paphiopedilum, 145
anatomy, 11
Anja 'Penny', HCC/AOS, **24**
armeniacum, 26
armeniacum 'Solar Max', **22**
barbatum, 24
bellatulum, 26
bellatulum 'Burmese Bell', AM/AOS, **23**
Betty Bracey 'Meadowlark', HCC/AOS, **24**
Bournhill, 18
callosum, 26
ciliolare, 21
delenatii, 26
delenatii 'Jillian', HCC/AOS, **22**
distribution, 19, 20, 22
Dollgoldi 'Golden Girl', AM/AOS, **26**
fairrieanum var. *album* 'Granny Smith', **21**
Gary Romagna 'Wizard's Fave', **27**
Green Gold, **24**
Green Window 'Stone', AM/AOS, **24**
Harrisianum, 24
henryanum 'Haley Suzanne', CCM/AOS, **2–3**
Iantha Stage 'Super,' **26**
insigne var. *sanderianum* 'Gladiator', AM/AOS, **21**
Irish Eyes 'Haley Suzanne', CCM/AOS, **25**
Magic Lantern 'Rose Glow', **26**
malipoense 'Bronstein-Walsh', AM/AOS, **22**
micranthum, 26
micranthum 'Afton', FCC/AOS, **22**
Parvisepalum group, 22
Petula 'Elaine's Booboo', HCC/AOS, **26**
philippinense, 20
rothschildianum, 26
rothschildianum 'Flying Wings', HCC/AOS, **20**
Sandra Bay, **24**
sukhakulii, 20, 21, 26
venustum, 20
victoria-regina, 20
villosum, 24
villosum 'Gold Moon', HCC/AOS, **21**
Paphiopedilum Alliance, 18–33
Parkinson, John, 8
Pelexia olivacea 'Adante', CBR/AOS, **112**
Peristeria, 130
elata, 122
elata 'Winged Beauty', CCM/AOS, **123**
Perreiraara Crownfox Agate 'Butter Baby', AM/AOS, **97**
Pescatorea lehmannii 'Passion', AM/AOS, **118**
pests, **146–147**
Phaius
tankervilleae 'Rabin's Raven', AM/AOS, **124**
tankervilleae 'Rosita', CCM/AOS, **125**
Phalaenopsis, 96, 108, 132, 143, 145, 146
amabilis, 99
amabilis 'Pamela's Perfection', AM/AOS, **100**
amboinensis, 106
anatomy, 10, 11
aphrodite, 104
bellina 'Herb's', **103**
Brecko Dreamcup 'Valle Mist', HCC/AOS, **107**
Brother Relaxed Fit 'Ontario Lava', HCC/AOS, **104**

Chiffon Angel 'Woody's Peloric', **105**
cornu-cervi, **102**
Dawn Treader, **104**
equestris, **104**
equestris 'Candor Violette', FCC/AOS, **102**
Everspring King 'Panda', JC/AOS, **106**
gigantea 'Mt. Vernon', AM/AOS, **102**
Glad Child 'Yamazato', AM/AOS, **104**
Golden Louis, **106**
Hilo Lip 'Lovely', 15, **104**
intermedia, **104**
leuddemanniana, **100**
lindenii, **100**
Malibu Minute 'Lisa', HCC/AOS, **104**
mariae, **102**
Mini Mark, **100**
Mini Mark 'Sara Michelle', AM/AOS, **106**
parishii, **100**, **106**
philippinensis 'Christina's Delight', AM/AOS, **101**
reichenbachiana 'orchidPhile', CBR/AOS, **102**
rosea, **104**
schilleriana, **99**
schilleriana 'Avi', CCM/AOS, **100**
schilleriana 'Lovely', AM/AOS, **100**
Sogo Lion 'Orchid World', HCC/AOS, **106**
Splish Splash 'Peloric No. 3', HCC/AOS, **98**
stuartiana 'Peter', HCC/AOS, **100**
Walden's Pumpkin Patch 'Orange Passion', AM/AOS, **106**
Wild Delight 'Travis', HCC/AOS, **104**
Zuma Jo 'Chadwick', HCC/AOS, **106**
Phalaenopsis Alliance, 98–109
Phragmipedium
    besseae, 30
    besseae 'Apricot', **28**
    besseae 'Eat My Dust', **28**
    besseae var. *flavum* 'Sundance', **28**
    caricinum, **28**
    China Dragon 'Elegant', **30**
    distribution, 19
    Don Wimber 'Penny', HCC/AOS, **30**
    Elizabeth March 'Lovely', **30**
    Eric Young, 30
    Eric Young 'Ethereal', **31**
    Grande, 30
    Jason Fischer 'Phoenix Rising', AM/AOS, **30**
    longifolium, 28, 30
    longifolium 'Lexie Sauer', AM/AOS, **4**, **28**
    Mem. Dick Clements 'Rich Red', HCC/AOS, **30**
    Noirmont 'Firebird', **30**
    pearcei, **28**
    sargentianum, 30
    schlimii, 30
    Sedenii, 30
    Sorcerer's Apprentice 'Lothar', AM/AOS, **30**
    wallisii 'White River Cascade', HCC/AOS, **28**
    wallisii 'Wintergreen', **29**
pink lady slipper, 32
Platystele minimiflora, **74**
Pleione formosana, **10–11**, **126**
Pleurothallid Alliance, **68–75**
Pleurothallids, 53, **68–75**
Pleurothallis, **145**
    dunstervillei 'Hoosier', CBR/AOS, **72**
    hamosa 'D & B', CHM/AOS, **72**
    niveoglobula, **72**
    paquishae 'Traders Point', CBR/AOS, **72**
Pliny, 8
Podangis dactyloceras, **136**
pollination strategies, 112, 114, 116, 134, 136
pollinia, 11
Polychilos, **102**
Polyradicion lindenii, **135**, **153**
pots, **143**
Power, Charles, 9
propagation, 9, **144**
Prosthechea baculus, **141**

Pteroceras appendiculata, **132**
Pterostylis abrupta, **112**

Q

queen lady slipper, **32**
"Queen of Flowers," 53

R

Rangaeris amaniensis 'Lauray', CCM/AOS, **136**
Renanthera, 96
    imschootiana, **92**
    monachica, **92**
    storiei, **92**
Renanthopsis Mildred Jameson, **96**
repotting, **143**
reproductive structures, 10–11, 38
Restrepia sanguinea 'Walter', **72**
Rhyncholaelia
    digbyana, 60
    digbyana 'Dragonstone', CCM/AOS, **66**
Rhynchostylis retusa, **92**
Rolfe, Robert A., 28
roots, **143**
rostellum, 11
Royal Botanic Gardens, Kew, 8
Ruíz and Pavón, 70

S

Saccolabium kotoense, **132**
Sander family, 9
Sarcochilus hartmannii 'England's Rose', HCC/AOS, **132**
scale insects (Boisduval), **146**
Schomburgkia splendida 'Roberto', AM/AOS, **66**
seeds, 9, **144**
Selenipedium, distribution, 19
sepal damage, **146**
Sheehan, Marion Ruff, 152
shows, **150–151**
Sideris, C. P., 94
slipper orchids, **32**
slugs, **146**
Smithsonian Institution, 6, 140
Sobraliinae, **126–127**
Sophrolaeliocattleya California Delight, **15**
Sophronitella violacea 'Fox Den', CCM/AOS, **67**
Sophronitis, 15
    coccinea 'Merilee', AM/AOS, **66**
Spiranthoideae, **112**
stamps, **5**, 152
Stanhopea barbata (*costaricensis*), **122**
Stanhopeinae, **122–123**
Star-of-Bethlehem orchid, **134**
Stenoglottis longifolia, **114**
Stenorrhynchos speciosum, **112**
Swainson, William, 9
Swartz, Olaf, 35, 42, 78

T

Tainia hookeriana, **124**
taxonomy, 12–13
temperature in cultivation, **145**
terrestrial media, **142**
Theophrastus, 8
Thouars, 128
thynnid wasp, **112**
Tiffany & Co., 152
Tokyo Dome Grand Prix Show, **151**
tree fern, **142**
Trichoglottis philippinensis var. *brachiata* 'Vin-Mar', AM/AOS, **133**
Tridactyle bicaudata, **136**
Trigonidium egertonianum, **122**

Trisetella hoeijeri, **74**
tulip orchids, 111, **120**

U

United States, orchid commerce in, 9, 35, 77, 82, 90

V

Vanda, 94, 96, 143, 145
    Bill Burke 'Redland Festival', CCM/AOS, **90**
    coerulea, 88, 90
    coerulea 'Evelyn', FCC/AOS, **88**
    coerulescens, 88, 90
    cristata, 90
    Crownfox Pink Glow 'Marie Daguia', AM/AOS, **90**
    denisoniana, 88, 90
    First and Last, 88
    First and Last 'Gladys Berrios', AM/AOS, **90**
    First and Last 'Hackneau's First Ten', HCC/AOS, **91**
    Gordon Dillon 'Memoria Khoi Truong', AM/AOS, **90**
    hookeriana, 90
    merillii, 87
    Miss Joaquim (*Papilionanthe* Miss Joaquim), 90
    Motes Buttercup 'Denise', AM/AOS, **90**
    Rose Davis 'Crownfox Snow', JC/AOS, **90**
    Rothschildiana, 88, 90
    roxburghii, 88
    sanderiana (*Euanthe sanderiana*), 88, 90
    sanderiana 'Chris', FCC/AOS, **88**
    Star Elite 'Memoria Vern Anderson', AM/AOS, **90**
    teres, 90
    tricolor, 90
    tricolor 'Summerland', HCC/AOS, **89**
    tricolor 'Viva Botanica', HCC/AOS, **88**
Vanda Alliance, **86–97**
Vandopsis gigantea, **132**
Vanilla, 8
vanilla scent/extract, 8
variability in orchids, **14–15**
varieties (botanical), 14
Vascostylis
    BonBon 'Fuchs Indigo', AM/AOS, **96**
    Crownfox Magic, **97**
    Cynthia Alonso 'Redland', HCC/AOS, **96**
    Precious 'Greta Von Krone', HCC/AOS, **96**
Vaughn, Lewis, 106
Veitch and Sons, 38
Veitch Royal Nursery, 24, 56, 62, 82, 104
viruses, **146**
von Linne, Carl, 32, 64
Vuylstekeara Linda Isler 'Montclair', HCC/AOS, **51**

W

Warrea, 118
watering, **145**
where to grow orchids, **148–149**
Wilder, Mr., 9
World Wildlife Fund, 140

Y

Young, Thomas, 9

Z

Zygoneria Adelaide Meadows 'Springtime', **119**
Zygopetalinae, **118–119**
Zygopetalum Syd Monkhouse 'Everglades', AM/AOS, **118**
Zygowarrea Springhurst 'JimLou', AM/AOS, **118**

ACKNOWLEDGMENTS

PICTURE CREDITS

The publishers would like to thank the following for their kind permission to reproduce the photographs:

Allikas, Greg: 4-5, 7, 44 cr, 50 bm, 53 tr, 55 c, 58 cl, 82 tl, 83, 87 tr, 90 tr, 90 cr, 90 bl, 94 tr, 94 cm, 95 , 96 cm, 96 bl, 96 br, 97 tl, 97 tm, 97 cl, 97 cr, 118 cl, 124 tl, 140 cr, 142 all except br, 143 (containers), 145 cr, 146 bl, 146 br, 148 tr, 148 cl, 148 bl, 150 (all), 152 br, 153; **American Orchid Society:** 5 tr, 8 tl, 19 tr, 33, 54 cl, 56 cl, 64 br, 66 bl, 94 br, 100 cm, 101, 106 tr, 106 br, 108 cm, 134 cm, 140 cl, 140 cm; **Baylis, Rebeca:** 78 bm; **Beckendorf, Steve:** 73; **Benzo, David M.:** 47 bl, 50 cr, 63 br; **Blooms of Bressingham:** 32 bm; **Brochu, M.D., Jean:** 55 br; **Bryan, Dave:** 63 br; **Clark, Richard:** 14 tr, 21 bl, 23, 30 bl, 39 tl, 55 bl, 56 cm, 57, 64 blm, 80 b, 108 tr, 118 br, 121 tm, 126 cl, 134 bl; **Coleman, Ronald A.:** 32 tr, 124 bl; **Corbis:** Franken, Owen 8bl, Cooke, Richard A. 9tl; **Crichton, Eric:** 50 tr, 82 bl, 88 brm, 126 bm; **Cuenca, Ramon:** 54 cr, 62 cl, 118 bl; **Cunningham, Billy:** Paulding Farnham: Tiffany's Lost Genius - Harry N. Abrams Publishers: 152 c; **Deifel, Joe:** 97 br; **DK Publishing:** 8 c,10-11 (center), 21 c, 60 bl, 126 cr, 144 cm; **Dressler, Kerry:** 74 cl, 112 tr, 112 cl, 113, 138-139, 141; **East, III, Bob:** 96 bm; **Ellsworth, Lewis:** 26 tr, 64 tr; **Fitch, Charles Marden:** 2-3, 9 br, 24 bl, 25, 30 br, 35 tr, 36 blm, 36 brm, 44 tr, 47 tl, 48 cm, 58 cr, 64 cl, 64 bl (inset), 67, 74 cr, 75, 78 br, 80 cl, 98-99, 102 bm, 102 br, 109 tr, 114 cm, 121 tr, 122 bl, 123, 127, 128 tr, 130 tr, 130 cr, 132, 136 cm, 136 blm, 136 br, 142 br, 143 tr, 143 (four in center), 144 tr, 144 cr, 144 (four on bottom), 145 cm, 146 cr, 147 b, 148cm, 148 cr, 148 bm, 148 br, 149; **Fleig, Richard E.:** 4 cl, 36 tr, 36 cr, 59, 64 brm, 108 br; **Fletcher, Neil:** 114 cr, 114 bl [Ophrys apifera]; **Fox, Jackie:** 106 cr; **Fujimoto, Dennis:** 84 brm; **Fulks, Gordon:** 5 bl; **Goo, Eric:** 108 cl; **Green, John:** 112 bl; **Hansknecht, Tom:** 84 bl; **Hermans, Johan:** 5 r, 16-17, 36 bl, 54 bm, 65, 72 cm, 72 brm, 74 tr, 74 cm, 74 bl, 74 bm, 74 cr, 77 tr, 78 tm, 78 bl, 80 cm, 80 cr, 88 cm, 88 bl, 92 tl, 100 tr, 102 cm, 116 tr, 116 cr, 116 bl, 122 tr, 122 cm, 126 bl, 128 cm, 129, 130 cl, 130 bm, 132 tr, 132 bl, 134 tr, 134 br, 136 tr, 136 cl, 136 bl, 136 brm, 137; **Herrington, Ann:** 14 cr; **Hia, Teck H.:** 32 cl; **Huber, Eldridge H.:** 38 cl, 66 tr; **Japan Gran Prix:** 151; **Johnson, Larry.:** 93, 94 cl, 106 cl, 125; **Keenan, Philip E.:** 32 cm, 32 br, 124 tr; **Kilfeather, Karen:** 109 tl; **Klehm, Julius:** 97 tr; **Kokin, Monroe:** 130 br, 132 cm; **Levy, Jo:** 42 tm; **Levy, Mrs. Ralph, Jr.:** 14 bl, 128 br; **Lewis, John H.:** 50 bl; **Mark, Buddy:** 36 cl; **Chuck McCartney:** 19 tr, 33, 135; **McCulloch, James E.:** 1, 4 cr, 28 cl, 42 bm, 55 tl, 69 tr, 70 cl, 70 br, 72 blm, 72 br, 80 tr, 100 bl, 109 br, 118 tr; **McLerran, Paul:** 88 tr; **Melendez, Mei Ling:** 82 br, 90 cm; **Miles, Karen Jensen:** 6 tl, 15 (all), 18-19, 20 tr, 20 cl, 20 bl, 21 tr, 24 tr, 24 tl, 24 cr, 28 bl, 28 bm, 38 tr, 38 bl, 42 tr, 42 cl, 42 bl, 43, 46 tr, 50 cl, 55 tr, 56 tr, 56 bl, 56 bm, 58 bl, 58 br, 60 tr, 60 cl, 60 bm, 60 br, 62 tr, 62 cr, 62 bm, 63 tl, 63 c, 63 bl, 66 cl, 76-77, 78 tl, 78 tr, 80 bl, 82 cr, 84 tr, 92 tm, 92 tr, 92 bl, 92 blm, 92 brm, 92 br, 96 tr, 100 bm, 102 cl, 112 bm, 116 cl, 116 br, 120 tr, 121 tr, 122 cl, 122 brm, 124 tm, 124 bm, 126 br, 128 cr, 130 cm, 132 cl, 132 blm, 132 br, 134 bm; **Miller, Alan J.:** 97 bl; **Nelson, John:** 22 cm, 44 br, 47 tr, 118 tm; **Norris, Jay:** 26 cl, 41 tr, 50 br, 68-69, 116 bm, 117; **Oakeley, Henry F.** 110-111, 120 cl, 120 tm, 120 bl, 120 bm, 120 br, 121 cl, 121 cr, 121 bl; **Okuhara, Sadao:** 58 tr, 104 bl; **Olsen, Huck:** 97 bm; **Osen, James:** 22 bl; **Otaki, Richard K.:** 20 br, 48 br; **Parker, J. M.:** 14 cm; **Paroly, Mitch:** 4 br, 24 br; **Peakall, Dr. Rod:** 112 cm; **Pendleton, Mark:** 21 tl, 22 tr, 26 bl, 26 br, 27, 28 tm, 28 tr, 28 cr, 29, 30 cl, 30 blm, 30 brm, 31, 36 br, 37, 38 blm, 38 brm, 39 tr, 39 cl, 39 cr, 39 bl, 39 br, 40-41, 44 bl, 46 cm, 46 bl, 47 c, 47 br, 48 cl, 48 bm, 49, 62 bl , 66 br, tr, 70 tr, 70 cm, 70 bl, 71, 72 tl, 72 tr, 79, 81, 84 blm, 84 br, 85, 100 cr, 100 br, 103, 104 cm, 104 bm, 105, 109 bl, 112 cr, 114 tr, 114 cl, 115, 119, 121 tl, 122 br, 124 tr, 126 tr , 128 cl, 131, 134 cl; **Peters, Rhonda:** 21 br, 52-53, 86-87, 106 bl, 111 tr, 112 br; **Peterson, David:** 58 bm, 146 tr; **Pinkers, Arthur T.:** 28 br, 30 tr, 99 tr, 109 cr, 109 bm; **Plank, Larry:** 100 cl; **Pruyn, S. C.:** 121 bm; **Randolph, Charlotte:** 56 cr; **R. F. Orchids, Inc.:** 96 cl, 97 cm; **Rowden, Charles:** 34-35, 38 br, 48 bl, 51, 64 cr, 82 tr, 89, 90 cl, 104 tr, 104 cl, 108 bm, 109 tm; **Royal Botanic Garden, Edinburgh:** 32 bl; **Ruger:** 114 blm, 114 brm, 114 br; **Sheehan, Marion Ruff:** 10-11 (all except center); **Siegler, Karl:** 48 tr, 90 br, 104 br; **Stewart, M.D., Robert:** 54 tr; **Stubbings, John:** 22 br; **Tauber, Richard:** 147 tr; **Teaf, Adrian R.:** 14 br; **Templeton, Richard:** 42 br; **Tinschert, Otto:** 54 bl; **Upton, Walter T.:** 80 bm, 130 bl; **Uribe, Juan Carlos:** 66 cm, 122 blm; **Usery, Butch:** 30 cr, 45, 61, 84 cr, 90 bm, 91, 107, 109 cl, 133; **Volpe, Joe:** 88 blm; **Vondersaar, Joe:** 102 tr; **Walters, Ernest:** 88 br; **Wilson, Donald F.:** 46 bm, 64 bl, 66 bm, 84 cl, 108 bl, 128 bl, 128 bm; **Wilson, Karen:** 72 bl, 94 bl.

Jacket credits

front cover: *Phalaenopsis equestris* 'Candor Violette', FCC/AOS, **Charles Marden Fitch**; front flap, top: *Paphiopedilum ciliolare*, **Karen Jensen Miles**; front flap, bottom: *Masdevallia* Charisma 'Keeno', **Mark Pendleton**; spine: *Paphiopedilum* Goultenianum 'Album', **Eric Crichton**; back, top left: *Cattleya aclandiae* 'Joe Elmore', HCC/AOS, **James E. McCulloch**; back, top left center: *Ascocenda* Crownfox Golden Dawn 'Miramar', AM/AOS, **Greg Allikas**; back, top right center: *Odontioda* Mount Bingham, **DK Publishing**; back, top right: *Cypripedium reginae*, **DK Publishing**; back, bottom: *Dendrobium* Momozono 'Princess', **Eric Crichton**.

AMERICAN ORCHID SOCIETY'S ACKNOWLEDGMENTS

Special thanks to American Orchid Society staff members Arlene Maguire, Susan Jones, Jane Mengel, Pam Giust, Ned Nash, Andy Easton and Sylvia Wood, and to the members of the Society's Conservation Committee, whose guidelines for conserving orchids are printed on page 140. The Society would also like to thank its gifted photographers for their portraits of orchids, and the talented growers whose horticultural skills brought the plants into flower so their beauty could be shared with others. Thanks also to Ronald A. Coleman, Kerry Dressler, Johan Hermans, Philip E. Keenan, Chuck McCartney, Dr. Henry F. Oakeley, Mark Pendleton, and R. F. Orchids, Inc. The glossary on pages 154–155 is adapted from the American Orchid Society's *Illustrated Orchid Dictionary* (2002 Revised Edition).

PUBLISHER'S ACKNOWLEDGMENTS

DK Publishing, Inc. would like to thank Jim Watson, Publications Director of the American Orchid Society, for his unfailing efforts in putting this book together. Similarly, DK would like to thank Ellen Nanney and Tom Mirenda of the Smithsonian Institution for their extremely valuable contributions. A special thank you to Greg Allikas for his custom digital photography and to Jonathan Bennett for his invaluable design assistance.

AMERICAN ORCHID SOCIETY

With 30,000 members and 550 Affiliated Societies worldwide, the American Orchid Society is the world's largest specialty horticultural organization. Since it was founded in 1921, the Society, a 501(c)(3) nonprofit scientific and horticultural organization, has extended the knowledge, production, use, perpetuation and appreciation of orchids. The Society is housed in the International Orchid Center, which features 3.5 acres of botanical gardens and greenhouses, with displays of orchids and exotic plants, in Delray Beach, Florida. Anyone with a passion for orchids is invited to visit the Society's orchid campus, where classes, displays and garden tours help the organization achieve its mission of providing global leadership in orchids. The Society maintains a popular Web site (orchidweb.org) that offers convenient access to a calendar of orchid events, lists of commercial growers and Affiliated Societies, and information on the cultivation and conservation of orchids.

Membership benefits include a subscription to the monthly magazine *Orchids*, a free copy of *Your First Orchid* to first-time members, *AOS Orchid Source Directory*, a 10 percent discount on items purchased in the Orchid Emporium and The AOS BookShop, and free admission to the International Orchid Center.

American Orchid Society
16700 AOS Lane
Delray Beach, Florida 33446-4351
Tel: 561-404-2000
Fax: 561-404-2100
E-mail: TheAOS@aos.org
Web site: orchidweb.org
Orchid Emporium and The AOS BookShop

Toll free: 1-877-ORCHIDS (672-4437) or 561-404-2020